SHIFT
A PLAYBOOK
FOR **POSITIVE** CHANGE

DOUGLAS M. WILLIAMS, JR.

I wish I had had this book earlier in my life. It would have catapulted me in my career by giving me a clear, competitive advantage. Doug's practical shifts in thinking and doing, coupled with great real life examples to make them accessible, gives anyone a full quiver of options when navigating and negotiating one's life and career. This is a must read.

Jimmy Leppert
Director, Kotter International;
Co-founder, Academy for Systems Change

Doug Williams' first book teaches us to make a shift in our perspective through this journey we call life. I found the reminder to "enjoy the walk" particularly powerful. All too often, we are focused on shallow goals, which even when met, fail to fulfill our true purpose.

This book is a practical guide as well as a deep, reflective read. We learn about the importance of WHY, a clarity which helps frame HOW we approach work and life. We next move from the theoretical to the intensely practical – tips for great presentations, effective listening skills, and having a team and service oriented approach versus shallow self-serving targets. After reading this book the first time, I was able to rethink some short-term goals. Soon, I will read it again to guide long-term goal setting.

Debjani Biswas
Internationally Bestselling Author of Miserably Successful
No More, #UsToo and Unleash the Power of Diversity

TABLE OF CONTENTS

CHAPTER 1

FINDING YOUR "WHY"

"When you know your WHY, you'll find your way."
—MICHAEL HYATT

"Without knowing what I am and why I am here,
life is impossible."
—LEO TOLSTOY

"The two most important days in your life are the day
you are born and the day you find out why."
—MARK TWAIN

Knowing your WHY is critical to finding success and fulfillment in life, no matter how you define it. Whether you are just starting out on your professional journey, are a mid-career executive, or you are nearing retirement and considering what the next chapter may hold for you, knowing your WHY will give you greater clarity, increased confidence, and more purpose for the next part of your journey.

In his book "The Power of Why: Breaking Out in a Competitive Marketplace," business consultant C. Richard Weylman writes,

> *If you ask why, then ask again, and then again, you can discover the truth about solving any problem in business. This works for every aspect of your company, from building a team to product development to sales and customer retention.*[1]

I would go a step further and suggest that following that advice can help you solve *any* problem you may experience in both your professional and personal life. Taking the time to dig deep and find out why that issue is happening, why you feel the way you do, why you acted the way you did, and why you said what you said will give you clarity and insight about what's really going on and how to handle it.

People Need Purpose

We all crave passion. As humans, we are meant for meaning. Zig Ziglar—a well-known motivational speaker, sales trainer, and writer—said, "Man was designed for accomplishment, engineered for success, and endowed with seeds of greatness."

We were made to be more than just "order takers." You are a creator, a leader, an influencer, and an important contributor to society. Success in life goes far beyond "name, rank, and serial number."

Start with Why

If you are feeling empty right now or are devoid of passion in your current work situation, I encourage you to ask yourself why. Why do you feel that way? Why aren't you doing something about it? Why are you not stepping into your greatness by doing what you are supposed to do?

Conversely, if you are totally satisfied in your life and career, then go ahead and ask yourself why as well. Why do you enjoy your work so much? Why are you so enthused about your job? Why don't you do more of it?

Regardless of how you feel—positive, negative, or ambivalent—answering the question "why" will give your life more meaning and a deeper understanding of your true wants and desires.

In the preface to his bestselling book "Start with Why: How Great Leaders Inspire Everyone to Take Action," Simon Sinek writes:

> *When I first discovered this thing called the WHY, it came at a time in my life when I needed it. It wasn't an academic or intellectual pursuit; I had fallen out of love with my work and found myself in a very dark place... I was no longer fulfilled by my work and I needed to find a way to rekindle my passion. The discovery of WHY completely changed my view of the world and discovering my own WHY restored my passion to a degree multiple times greater than at any other time in my life. It was such a simple, powerful, and actionable idea, that I shared it with*

my friends. That's what we do when we find something of value; we share it with the people we love. Inspired, my friends started making big life changes. In turn, they invited me to share this idea with their friends, the people they loved. And so the idea started to spread... The more organizations and people who learn to also start with WHY, the more people there will be who wake up feeling fulfilled by the work they do. And that's about the best reason I can think of to continue sharing this idea.[2]

Have you discovered your WHY? Are you fulfilled and passionate about what you do? Based on the answers to these questions, what is it you need to do next?

How Zig Ziglar Made Me Curious About Life

When I was younger, I started a company that provided software for physicians to use in billing their patients. I created the business from scratch and did everything from writing software to calling on doctors. I really needed to learn everything I could about selling.

I had to understand how to fill a sales pipeline, how to call on prospects and clients, how to create relationships, how to do quality follow up, and how to make sure I asked open-ended questions.

Again, Zig Ziglar, master sales trainer, came to the rescue. I read everything of his I could get my hands on including "See You at the Top," "Secrets of Closing the Sale," and "Born to Win."

Reading Ziglar taught me a lot about the urgency of selling and the importance of selling. I learned about the need to build relationships, how to prepare my opening comments, as well as how to structure a conversation. Immersing myself in Ziglar's philosophies opened a new way of seeing the world that I just hadn't seen before.

> For me, this whole learning process started with Ziglar's books. He really cemented why it is important to read self-help books, and why it's important to keep reading for personal and professional development, and how to stay curious throughout life. It's very important to keep learning at any age. Though I am 60 years old as I write this book, I still find myself amazingly curious.

With the Internet right in front of you all day long, there is almost a limitless range of topics you can learn about. Anything you ever want to know is on the web. Whether you want to master tying a nautical knot, speak a new language, or learn about depreciation, the world of information is at your fingertips. There's much to learn that will add value to you professionally and bring enjoyment to you personally.

Peter Senge, Grand Pianos, and a Change of Perspective

One of the benefits of learning new things is that it allows you to see the world from different perspectives. I was reminded of the power of perspective while consulting at the accounting giant Arthur Andersen. Peter Senge, author of the bestselling business classic "The Fifth Discipline: The Art and Practice of the Learning Organization,"came in to help us learn how to see things from a different perspective when trying to solve an especially perplexing problem.

One of the first activities his team led us through required a grand piano and comfortable clothes. First, they had us lie under the piano while someone played it. Then we listened from directly above it. Then off to the side. It was amazing how different the music sounded depending on where we were when listening. The perspective from under a grand piano is different from being above it or next to it. The activity clearly showed the importance of seeing things, or—in this case—hearing them, from different perspectives.

Making the Shift

The exercise with the piano helped my team see the importance of being open to a shift in perspective. You may be asking,"What does perspective have to do with the "why" of my life?" I'm glad you asked. Problem solving is a big part of the human experience. Being aware of why you see things the way you do—especially when addressing challenges—and then considering the perspectives of others, increases the potential for positive outcomes. I hope you'll use the following pages as your playbook for making the shift toward positive change.

Who Does It Help?

This book is designed to help you in your life, your career, and your relationships. For instance, active listening will continue to pay benefits on many of your relationships forever. Learning how to assume the best in the people you interact with not only changes you, it can change the other person.

The great thing about this book is you don't have to devour it all at once, it can be read in small doses. Pull the book out when you need it, or when you think it will be useful for the people on your team. You can work through the book by yourself as you try to improve in specific areas, or you can work through it with a friend or family member. The important thing is just to get started.

CHAPTER 2

WHY TO TRY:

Thomas Edison, Eighteen-Wheelers and Finding Your Purpose in Life

"Life is about taking chances, trying new things, having fun, making mistakes and learning from it."
— ANONYMOUS

"If you never did, you should. These things are fun and fun is good."
— DR. SEUSS

Have you ever tried something new and failed? Sure, we all have. Failing is a natural part of the learning process.

I have always loved the story of Thomas Edison and his invention of the carbonized filament for the incandescent light bulb. As the story goes, when asked by a reporter what it felt like to have failed a thousand times, Edison simply replied that he had not failed, but had learned 999 ways that didn't work. What a great attitude to have for life!

Thomas Edison was quite the inventor and certainly made his contributions to humanity. By the time he invented the light bulb, he already had a long entrepreneurial history, which is confirmed by the fact that, over his lifetime, Edison acquired 1,093 patents!

One of the keys to Edison's success, in addition to his positive re-framing of failure as a learning experience, was his insatiable desire to try new things. For instance, of his 1,000-plus patents, history.com reports that "389 were for electric light and power, 195 were for the phonograph, 150 for the telegraph, 141 were for storage batteries, and 34 patents were for the telephone."[1]

Edison was certainly a guy who knew how to experiment with new ideas, and he learned from his mistakes. Can you imagine if he had been afraid to try new things? Just think—you may have had to read this book by candlelight. Where have you failed and believe you can't do it better the next time? More importantly, what have you learned from failing that could make you successful next time?

Write down the lesson learned from your latest setback/failure.

A more modern yet equally inspirational story of inventiveness is the genesis story behind Airbnb, the online accommodation service that "Lets users stay anywhere from a couch to a castle."[2]

In 2008, three roommates—Joe Gebbia, Nathan Blecharcyk, and Brian Chesky—launched a simple website to help them rent out their San Francisco apartment for the weekend. In doing so, the trio unintentionally jump-started the worldwide "sharing economy."

Their idea was born out of desperation—they were simply looking for a way to pay their rent. But that first weekend, the roommates ended up hosting three different house-guests and made about $1,000. Convinced they were onto something, the unintentional entrepreneurs carried on with their newfound business plan. In 2009, after failing several times to secure funding, they finally landed a $600,000 seed investment from Sequoia Capital and Y Ventures.[3]

Over the last decade, Airbnb has grown from a small online startup to a global phenomenon with over six million listings in 191 countries. With an average of more than 500,000 stays across the world per night, IProperty Management reports this accommodation powerhouse has a valuation of over $35 billion dollars. Airbnb's major asset isn't even tangible, it's merely connecting people who have a need with people who can supply it. This was an idea born out of necessity.

Any ideas you have not acted on? Write them down here; don't judge, just write.

_____

_____

_____

_____

_____

_____

I love these stories because they speak to the importance of trying new things. In the case of Thomas Edison, he was a serial inventor who had a goal of coming up with at least one minor invention everyday. In the case of Airbnb, the business model was really created out of the founders' need to pay rent. In each case, the catalyst (Edison and the three roommates-turned-billionaires) created worldwide breakthroughs and in the process *found* their passion for life. Each of them were in the moment and trying to meet a need. They weren't just going numbly to the next meeting or event, they were actively thinking.

In these stories, it was their ingenuity and creativity that enabled them to succeed. Even if you don't have dreams of becoming an international inventor or entrepreneur, I hope the tales of Edison and Airbnb will encourage you to explore new things. After all, you never know what kind of new opportunities await you! I believe there are opportunities right in front of you. If you just look for them, you will see them, and then you can write your own success story.

Why You Should Try New Things

When you were a little kid and your parents told you to try a new food or to eat all your dinner, and you refused, they probably came back with, "Well how do you know you don't like it if you don't try it?" It may sound like a silly example, but it's true. You may actually find that, just as you discovered new and delicious cuisine as a child, you enjoy doing things as an adult that you'd never expected to.

> Whether you're young or entering a transition period, it's important to explore many different outlets and try new things. You never know which areas you'll show competence or an interest in. What do you find yourself doing or thinking about in your down time? That could give you a clue as to your real passion.

It's the same way when you're starting your career or considering an internship in college. Sometimes you may not know what your next step will be. That's why it is important to always remain flexible and to begin getting comfortable with the *"uncomfortability"* of trying new things.

Every journey starts with the first step, so go ahead and take it. In today's market, change is the only constant, so learn to thrive in uncomfortable situations. In fact, I think that being uncomfortable may be the new normal in business, just as change is the new constant.

How will you ever know what you like and dislike in your life, education, or career if you don't try new things? How will you ever discover where your passion is if you don't really go out on a limb every once in a while? Who knows, you just might like that mustard-flavored milkshake after all.

Negotiating for a Win-Win

Trying new things and "getting comfortable with uncomfortability" is how I discovered that one of my favorite things to do in life is to negotiate with a client. The reason I love it so much is the same reason almost everybody else hates it: it's hard work. Sure, there's a lot of prep to do beforehand. To do a good job at negotiating, you must understand the other side and what they want and need. Traditional thinking holds that if it's a good negotiation, then both parties feel as if they've lost something. My hope in each negotiation is that both sides will feel as if they have won. Here's a hint: the fewer the people at the table, the faster you will come to agreement, and if you don't know what the person across the table calls success, you're already at a disadvantage.

Do you want to know how I came to realize that I love negotiating? I tried it. I just tried it. At first, I was horrible. I either just caved in or cut the difference in half, and then neither side felt good about it. There are a lot of things that people are interested in, but they may be too afraid to try because of how other people might view them from the outside. In reality, that should be the last thing on your mind. If you want to try something, don't let the fear of criticism or actual criticism hold you back. What if Edison had stopped after the first try, or what if his friends had said, "Really, Thomas? 250 tries and it still doesn't work?"

You may find that you fall in love with the "new thing," much as I did with negotiating. May be you'll enjoy it so much you commit to doing it for the rest of your life. Ok, that may be a bit of an overreach, but maybe you don't avoid it either. After a negotiation with a big client in which both sides were excited about the outcome, the opposing spokesman asked if I could come to the car dealer with him and help negotiate in the purchase of a new car! I took that as a positive!

Is there a reason not to continue to try new things, to open your mind to new horizons, to explore new opportunities? What will happen if you put yourself out there and try something new? If it doesn't work, or you make a mistake, then be like Edison and chalk it up to a learning experience.

Name three things you want to try: Quick, off the top of your head, write them down: _____

_____

_____

_____

_____

_____

_____

Stretching Your Capabilities

Trying new things will add to your arsenal of skills. But just as with physical stretching, stretching yourself by meeting new opportunities head on can be, well, a stretch. For example, how many of you hate public speaking? I used to hate it too. And it didn't matter the format or size of the group. I stutter, not all the time, but with P's and D's most of the time. And yes, my name is Doug, so sometimes just introducing myself can be a struggle!

When I started public speaking, I was "that guy." You know, the one who has 50 Power Point slides with hundreds of words on each. I would just stand there like a talking head, going "blah, blah, blah," even though the audience could read everything I was going to say. To top it off, I would turn from time to time and look at the slide, completely losing eye contact with my audience.

In order to stretch my capabilities as a speaker, I engaged a speech writer—a rather famous one, at that—and transitioned to using 100 percent pictures on my slides. Even when I speak today, there are never more than seven words per slide because I want people to focus on the concept that I'm teaching or the point I'm making. I want them to listen to me and *not* try to read ahead by focusing on the words on the slide. In fact, during a recent discussion on leadership excellence, I used one slide—a picture of a state-of-the-art catamaran—to make my point. In a sales meeting with over 120 people in attendance, I spoke for 20 minutes using only one slide as a backdrop because I really wanted the audience to catch the moment.

I've learned how to make data on a Power Point interesting by telling a story about why the information is helpful to my audience. I'll ask them reflective questions like "Why are you looking at this slide?" "Why are you listening to me now?" and "Why is this going to be important to you later?" As I get the audience to start considering my topic, they become more engaged, and then a meaningful conversation can emerge.

When I was the head of the healthcare consulting branch of a global company, I would regularly speak to large audiences. I would go out on stage and speak to people about technology, the future of technology, where the world is headed, and how it could affect their health-care business.

Sometimes, I would start my presentation with a video clip from "The Matrix" movie, by asking them right away, "Do you want to take the red pill or the blue?" and "Do you want to go back to sleep or do you want to know what the hell is really going to happen?"

It would literally stop the audience in their tracks. I would continue by asking them, "Okay, everybody who wants me to give the usual boring type of presentation with a big idea and a normal sale pitch, raise your hand. And now everybody who wants to actually think outside the box, raise your hand."

There was always a pause, followed by a group decision from the audience right then and there that pulled them into my presentation. Obviously, after an introduction like that not many of them wanted to hear the old standard stuff. They all wanted me to stretch their noggins. They wanted to learn and be somewhat entertained at the same time. That would be the type of presentation I would launch into for them.

With that one opening question, I had captivated their attention. I played it up by pausing and then walking around the stage in silence, just staring at them, quietly waiting for their reply. After that, I knew that for the next 45 minutes, I would have them in the palm of my hand, and I could help them be in the moment, learn, reflect, think......
otherwise, it would have been just another boring meeting.

It is a very effective way to grab their attention right from the start. At each of these events, everyone in the audience would lean in to hear me talk. They were all curious about what I was going to say next.

Stretching your capabilities can be as simple as taking something you are already doing today, like I did with presenting, and doing it a little bit differently; try something new or improve upon a technique. People come up to me years after hearing one of my talks and tell me they remembered the picture and what I had said… when that happens, it's amazing.

Do you remember the last presentation you attended? Or better yet, did someone comment on your last presentation? Write down your memories here.

_____

_____

_____

_____

_____

_____

_____

Thinking Differently Makes Others Think Differently About You

Anybody can apply this lesson, regardless of their field or area of study. I was just talking to a financial analyst the other day as he was doing spreadsheets for some financial models. He was doing the tactical job of modeling an acquisition to understand the entire financial picture. He'd done such modeling a hundred times before, but this time I asked him to look at things a little differently.

I talked to him about the proposed acquisition that he had modeled, and then I asked him to consider the additional capabilities of the acquisition as well as broader markets that weren't in the original business case.

"What if we were able to turn this deal from $25 million into $50 million in cash?" I asked. "How much more is possible if we drive this endeavor to reach its full potential?" When challenged about doing things the way he'd always done them, the analyst started looking at different ways to think about mergers and acquisitions that can affect the outcome of a deal.

Where once his coworkers looked at him as a bean counter, they now see him as someone who thinks outside the box. The analyst's new perspective caused his colleagues to have a new perspective of him. In the future, they will think of him as someone who can consider different perspectives and new ways of structuring deals. Not to mention, the whole process is a lot more fun for everyone.

Just Jump In and Say Yes

When I was going to school, I got a summer job for a delivery company unloading trucks—big trucks. When one truck was unloaded, we'd back up the next and continue unloading. I was paid to unload, but I loved to drive!

These vehicles were large 18-wheelers, so they were very hard to back up. After watching the others struggle to back up these trucks for about a month, I asked if I could try it.

I nailed it my first time. I was a natural. In fact, I could drive an 18-wheeler backwards better than some of the other people could drive them *forward*. I loved doing this. On some nights, I would even rearrange the truck fleet— in part so we could be more efficient in loading and unloading the next day—but also because I just really wanted to drive the big trucks. I loved everything about them: the buttons, sounds, diesel engine, and the mass of them. It was awesome.

One day, the company needed a load to be dropped off downtown at a very tight dock. Having seen my skills in the yard, the boss allowed me to drive the truck for the delivery. I pulled the truck into the dock perfectly on the first try. From then on, I was the guy they called on to do this type of precise driving. On those days, I got out of loading and unloading them, so it was a win-win!

A few weeks into the summer, after a long day of unloading trucks, we needed to take a load from Los Angeles to Phoenix. None of the drivers wanted to do it, so I volunteered, and, surprisingly, they let me!

Backing into my Future

I loved driving the big trucks so much that I eventually got my Commercial Driver's License—I became a real truck driver. This new skill helped me pay for college. One day I had to make a delivery at a dock that was very complicated. In fact, the staff at the warehouse used to watch to see how many times it took a driver to back his truck in, and then cheer if he or she ever got it square to the dock. Well, I hit it the first time, and everyone cheered. After months of delivering computers to this dock, the company manager I was delivering to offered me a job and paid me to become a computer technician!

The point is: one thing leads to another, so enjoy the journey. You never know what kind of doors may open for you as a result of trying new things. It's been 35 years since I learned how to back up trucks and work with computers. But I still love doing both today. Especially working with technology. It moves so fast and is always changing. It continues to present new challenges, just like life.

That's why being able to try new things is so important. It allows you to continually learn, grow, and update your skills so you become more valuable to others. Guess what, I can still easily back up a large truck, trailer, boat or camper perfectly on the first try! Now that's a skill that I know I will continue to use.

CHAPTER 3:

HOW TO ENJOY LIFE IN THE MOMENT

*"Joy does not simply happen to us.
We have to choose joy and keep choosing it every day."*
—HENRI J. M. NOUWEN

*"Choosing joy is being able to see God's goodness
even when life is hard and messy."*
—ANONYMOUS

*"When anxiety was great within me,
your consolation brought me joy."*
—PSALM 94:19, NIV

The sales this month are not going well. To make matters worse, I had left the house after a disagreement with my wife, and a driver cut me off on the way to work. Furthermore, I got caught by a train, which made me 15 minutes late for a very important meeting. Here I was, completely frustrated, and I had only been at work for five minutes!

Do you ever have a day that starts out like that? If so, this chapter is for you!

Learning how to enjoy life in the moment is critically important. Unfortunately, many people never learn it. This can be the difference between going through life with a sense of joy and purpose or being miserable. Without this key lesson, we are left to the whims of the day, our bosses, spouses, kids, or that jerk on the road. Life is too short for all this frustration. You can take back control of your life and emotions and experience true joy at all times.

I believe there is always a silver lining regardless of the situation. I know that life can be difficult. We live in a sinful and broken world. And sometimes situations may be so difficult that it's almost impossible to see the good in them or to be joyful.

But the truth is joy is an "inside" job. Here's what I mean. Real joy has less to do with your *outside* circumstances or environment, and more to do with the choices and decisions *inside* of you. When you come to this realization, it's easier to have the faith and confidence needed to choose joy in any circumstance.

The Difference between Joy and Happiness

There is a difference between joy and happiness. Joy is an inner peace that you develop and control. Happiness is more externally related and situationally based. Happiness is more surface level; it's more superficial. Happiness is more about emotions and can be fleeting or dependent upon something else. There's nothing wrong with happiness or finding things that make you happy, it's just important not to put your identity, or all of your hope and trust in happiness.

You can think of things that make you happy as a form of entertainment or as a reward. For example, eating a Chicago-style, deep-dish pizza might make me happy on a Friday night, but that's not where I find my identity. Neither do I find it in activities like golf, wine tasting, cycling, riding Harleys, or running. Those are just things I do that bring me a deep feeling of satisfaction and help change my focus.

Joy, on the other hand, is about a deeper inner peace. It's an attitude of the heart. For instance, oftentimes I'm not very happy when I'm driving on the freeway or I'm stuck in traffic. If I'm honest, I also tend to get pretty upset when someone cuts me off. But I don't let what happens on the road affect my attitude for the day. After I get to the office, I try to exhibit joy and share that joy with those around me. I'll ask my coworkers how they are doing that morning or how their evening was. I may ask them if they need me to do anything for them, or if there's anything major on their agenda that we need to talk about.

I walk around the office and talk to everyone and attempt to bring a smile to their faces. An important part of that is to stop and take the time to look them in the eye, showing that I acknowledge them and that they're important to me. These people are very important to me, not just for business, but because they are people. People can sense how you feel about them by the way you greet and treat them.

Have you taken a minute today to brighten someone's day? Who was it and what did you do to brighten their day?

_____

_____

_____

_____

_____

_____

The bottom line is, you can wake up and say, "This is how I'm setting my tone for the day. I'm going to choose to be joyful." Then you can share that joy with others. <u>The key is that joy is not based on a feeling, but on a decision.</u>

What about you? Have you made your decision today? What situations have you experienced in life where it was hard for you to find joy in the moment? Are there moments from the past that, as you sit back and look at them over the longer term, you can see how they actually helped you, stretched you, or grew you in ways you may not have otherwise experienced? Do you feel anxious or depressed, or are you worried that bad things could happen to you? Try to project to the future and consider how your current situation could actually be a great learning experience.

How are you feeling now? What can you do to change the way you feel, if necessary?

_____

_____

_____

_____

_____

_____

_____

A Deep Gladness—Even in Difficulty

When addressing the difference between joy and happiness, theologian and pastor Christopher Benek put it like this:

> *"Joy, on the other hand, is at least grounded in the idea that something is good for someone else. We have joy when — even in our suffering — we are acting toward someone else's wellbeing… If you have ever selflessly given of yourself or that which you own, you are certainly familiar with this feeling. We experience joy when we achieve selflessness to the point of personal sacrifice...We feel joy when we are spiritually connected to God or people."[1]*

This is why the Biblical writer of Hebrews was able to say, "Let us fix our eyes on Jesus, the author and perfecter of our faith, who for the joy set before him endured the cross..." (Hebrews 12:2a). How wonderful is that? It is both amazing and mind-boggling. I mean, really, crucifixion was torture. In fact, crucifixion was normally reserved for the worst prisoners in the Roman Empire.

So how was it that the writer of Hebrews could say such a thing? It's because of the message of the Gospel: "God loved us so much, that he gave his only son so that we might have eternal life" (John 3:16). Of course, Jesus didn't stay dead. He conquered the grave in order to receive his prize—his Bride, the Church. Jesus endured the cross for the deep gladness he found in giving us eternal life through our relationship with him. Be joyful, God offers it to everyone.

This is where I get my joy, where do you get yours?

_____

_____

_____

_____

_____

_____

_____

Keep a Positive Attitude and Assume Positive Intent

One great way to reinforce making the decision to stay joyful everyday is to keep a positive attitude. Whenever you're interacting with somebody, always try to keep a positive attitude and assume they have positive intent towards you. Be conscious of how you approach people. Be aware of the tone of your voice when you talk to them, the way you smile, any facial expressions you make, and any body language you may be projecting. Though these may be subtle actions, people can get a sense from you that you're a positive person. When they feel that, they'll be more apt to talk to you and will include you more often in their life and work. It's just more fun to be around a positive person. Think about your friends and who you hang around with. Are they pumping you up or inviting you into their problems?

If I'm positive, and someone says to me, "Hey, you have something between your teeth," I'm not going to be grouchy about it. I won't be offended, because I'm going to assume positive intent. I'll reply to them by saying, "Hey, thanks. I really appreciate that." I certainly don't want to be embarrassed in a meeting later on because I have asparagus hanging out of my mouth. I'm glad they told me. Thank them for their willingness to put your best ahead of their feelings of awkwardness in telling you.

It's the same if someone corrects you in a business conversation, or they give you some coaching in another area. The point is if you assume positive intent, you will receive positive intent. And think about it, if that person did not care, why would they tell you? It takes courage to tell someone something constructive rather than being silent. Help others, <u>life is not a zero-sum game</u>, we all have lots to learn and to offer! Always do it from a positive perspective.

Being positive and assuming positive intent go hand in hand. You might just find that when you adopt this kind of outlook, it makes life more enjoyable and the world a lot friendlier.

Learning How to Enjoy the Moment in an Instant Gratification Culture

Some people have trouble just sitting back and enjoying the process. They get too impatient, or they want to receive the benefit without having first put in the work. Life is like a marathon, not a sprint. People fail to see that the journey to success in life is more like the process of a crockpot or slow cooker—not a microwave. It takes time to reach your goals.

We live in an instant gratification culture where everyone wants everything now. That kind of mentality often is at odds with the way life works. I know people who can't go five minutes without checking their phones—even when driving! And I told you, I'm a stickler for driving (remember my truck story from Chapter 2?).

When I'm driving, I don't even look at my phone. I'm just not that interested. I don't care if it beeps at me 25 times. It can wait. I just don't care. Instead, I'm focused on the road and driving. Or if it's a nice day, I may be looking out the window at the cows in the field or the flowers alongside the road or whatever.

The point is, I take time to enjoy the moment, and I don't need to be distracted every five seconds. I don't need the rush of a chemical reaction in my brain from the endorphins released when I check my phone. That kind of instant gratification just doesn't appeal to me. How many times have you checked your phone in this chapter? Try to go a whole chapter or two without checking, I promise, life won't end, and you will get more out of the chapter!

If it's an emergency, they will call back or leave a message. Otherwise, most things can wait until I have a dedicated time to offer a reply. If I don't respond to a text message or email right away, it's not the end of the world. Life goes on, and I'm going to enjoy it in the process. Try something: drive to work and don't look at your phone. Then, in the afternoon, take 10 minutes to check it when you get home from work and don't look at it again the rest of the night. Instead, say hi to your family and greet everyone in the house, not just the pets!

Smile, Breathe, and Relax

When difficult things do happen, or challenges come up, the best thing to do is to pause, breathe, and relax. Try not to stress out too much. Just sit back and find a way to smile. There's a silver lining in it somewhere.

Try to look for the deeper meaning behind the challenge. Ask yourself why this could be happening to you. If you are spiritual, try to have enough faith to trust God and believe that things will work out.

I don't mean when you're in a really tough situation you force a fake grin on your face. That's not what I'm talking about. Sometimes you may only be able to smile on the inside. And that's ok too. You can have an attitude that says, *I'm going to get through this. I will learn something here. Even if I don't understand this, I'm going to use it to benefit myself and others somehow.* When we encounter a struggle, it often just means that God has a different door he wants us to go through. Or maybe there's a different opportunity for us that we are not aware of.

I remember one time at work we were having a terrible quarter. It was probably the worst quarter in our business's history. Our stock plummeted. Everyone was stressed. All the executives were frantically pulling out their charts, while they watched investors pulling out of our stock on the screen. Both our company's profitability and morale shot straight to the bottom. It was horrible.

And it was during that down time when I looked at my CFO one day, gave him the old Scooby Doo *"Ruh Roh,"* and smiled. He said that's when he knew we were going to make it. That same CFO came up to me later and said, "I just want to tell you why I like working with you. Because you're not scared in this business. And when you said 'Ruh Roh,' I looked at you and thought, 'You know what, you and I are going to be friends.'" And we made it through that quarter and many after that! He is a great CFO, and we do like working together.

My lightheartedness didn't dismiss the seriousness of the situation, it just made it more bearable. I kept my joy and humor in a difficult time, and I was able to make others smile in the process. That's what I mean about learning to smile and breathe during tough times. I believe if you can relax, look at the bright side and take a moment, you will make better decisions and perform much better than if you are consumed by stress.

Bad things are going to happen to you; how you respond to those bad things matters. It not only matters to you, it also matters to the people around you. The more senior of a leadership role you grow into, the more people will look to you as an example. They will weigh their emotions and reactions based on yours. Again, try to stay positive and keep your joy as a light for others to follow. Make the first comment out of your mouth be a constructive or insightful one, not one of negativity or panic. It does matter.

Joy through Grief and Loss

In 2017 I unexpectedly lost my son, Cameron. He was just 28 years old. And it was hard. It was hard for me. It was hard for his mom and his sister. It was hard for everyone who knew him. Cameron was a great kid.

Cameron was a free spirit. He had a contagious and friendly personality. In his short life, he had an impact on many people. He was an excellent musician, having played both drums and bass guitar. He was also a great freelance bartender. Cameron just didn't blend in well with the rest of society. He hated "the man." And he absolutely hated the idea of having a nine-to-five job.

I didn't know Cameron had been struggling with alcohol, because we lived in different states. He lived with his sister in California, and I lived in Texas. When it finally came out that he was an alcoholic, he decided to do something about it. He went to rehab in North Carolina because he didn't want to go in Cali, and he hated the idea of having a parental figure present if he went in Texas.

Since he had friends in North Carolina, he did rehab there. He actually got clean for 30 days. After he exited rehab, he was living in a halfway house. I was planning to go see him, to make sure that he knew I loved him, but when I called, his counselor told me to wait because Cameron was processing things. She said he felt kind of angry with me. She said she thought it was an anger borne of a fear of letting me down. So, I didn't go.

I'm thankful though because I still got to talk to him literally a day or two before he passed away. In my last conversation with him, he said, "Dad, I love you." I knew he did, and I answered, "Cameron, I love you too. I can't wait to come out and see you."

During that conversation, we talked about drugs, and he said that he'd never done drugs. I naively believed him, so when he overdosed within days, I was beyond shocked. Evidently, Cameron got some sort of a street-based opioid that contained fentanyl. That stuff is as strong as an elephant tranquilizer. Basically, he took it, fell asleep and stopped breathing.

You always ask yourself when somebody you love passes away, "What could I have done differently?" If it's your parents or your grandparents you might think, "Should I have spent more time with them? Could I have been there in the end? Is there anything else I could have helped them with?" You know, those kinds of things just cross your mind.

I questioned "Was I too hard on him? Was I too soft? Was his death a byproduct of my parenting?" I had all these unanswered questions. As a Christian, I believe that God is in control and that there must have been a bigger purpose in mind, even if I don't understand it.

I don't sit up at night and worry that my parenting killed my son. That's not something I think about. I am sad that my son passed. But I still have my joy because I believe that Cameron is in a better place. I have joy because I know one day I'll see him again.

What situations have you experienced in life? Are there challenges you have worried about today? What areas of stress do you have where the silver lining eludes you? Where can you choose to be joyful today, even in the face of

difficulty or loss? Joy is a choice and—with faith in God—
that choice can be strengthened today.

_____

_____

_____

_____

_____

_____

CHAPTER 4

THE POWER OF FOCUS

"Focus. Otherwise you will find life becomes a blur."
—ANONYMOUS

"Always remember, your focus becomes your reality."
—GEORGE LUCAS

"The main thing is to keep the main thing the main thing."
— STEPHEN R. COVEY

The power of focus is paramount. A great example is the focus of a pilot. We need them to focus, right? I have logged about 500 hours flying airplanes. I am complex and instrument rated. Let me elaborate. A complex airplane has landing gear that you put up and down. You never want to land your plane with the gear up—it's bad, very bad. Because of that, airplane manufacturers have put a loud horn in the airplane to remind you, as the pilot, to deploy your gear while landing. If your airspeed gets below a certain level and your altitude is at a certain level, the horn will come on to alert you to the fact that your gear is not down.

I can't even tell you the number of times I've read about pilots who landed with their gear up. They all say the same thing—they couldn't concentrate because there was a loud horn going off in their ear! Ironic, right? This focus, or disruption thereof, is indicative of what often happens in life. Too many people live their lives like those pilots—focusing on the wrong things and totally missing the important ones.

Being In the Moment

So many people have trouble learning how to just "be" in the moment. Our society today is designed around an overload of stimuli. There's just too much noise and distraction available. For example, we use screens on nearly all of our electronics. The beeps and buzzes from our phones, cars, computers, and security cameras, among other things, all constantly interrupt our lives.

Sure, these interruptions allow us to switch topics quickly and "multi-task." But as a result, we typically only stay at the surface level. These interruptions may be for good things or something that demands our attention. We might be afraid we'll miss something if we don't reply right away, but all too often, these distractions don't do us any good.

For instance, at work, people constantly text me. I have people on my computer instant messaging me. I get all kinds of phone calls at three- or four-minute intervals. So how do I stay present and in the moment with the person I am talking to? How do I stay on task during the meetings I'm in, and how do I stay productive throughout the rest of the day? The answer is the **power of focus.**

Focus on What Matters

Focus allows us to go deep and ask the next question. When we focus, we are able to reveal our true and innermost feelings. Focus allows us to force ourselves to slow down, to think deeply, and to understand what really drives us. This will allow you to focus on what really matters. Once you can focus enough to find out what drives you today, you will be able to start building a better life for tomorrow. That's the way to ensure that you create the life you want and the one that will be the most fulfilling for you.

I remember hearing a story from Zig Ziglar. He was talking about when he sold cooking pans early in his career. His story was fascinating. He said one day he got so caught up in the sales presentation with a homeowner that he forgot about another appointment he had set up across town.

The woman in front of him was ready to buy all of his pans, but all Zig could think about was getting out of there and heading over to the next appointment before he was too late. Talk about a lack of keeping the main thing *the main thing*! In reality, he should have stayed there with the first woman and closed the sale because that was the whole point of what he was trying to do in the first place. Don't lose sight of the goal. The key is to be fully present in the moment and focus on what matters most.

It reminds me of a funny story told by my son-in-law.

The first tidbit of advice that Doug shared with me changed my life. And it was delivered within an hour of meeting me—his future son-in-law. "Life is short," he said. "The most important question you can ask yourself while here on earth is simple. It's 'Why?'"

A few minutes prior to talking with her father, Victoria and I were seated around a dinner table in downtown Austin with her family celebrating her graduation from UT. After a cocktail or two, Victoria's mom asked the table who wanted to give the toast. Being the new guy, I volunteered (in effort to break the ice), although I had nothing clever or cute lined up. My stomach dropped and my face went pale as I looked at Victoria. I had literally just met her family, so she was nervous to begin with. When she saw in my eyes that I was about to go "off script" and wing it, she went pale too. I raised my glass, and the table followed suit as I proceeded to recite the last toast I had heard—at a frat house dinner.

Silence. For a full 30 seconds. A "one-Mississippi, two-Mississippi..." type of 30 seconds. By the 15-second mark, I had completely lost feeling in my right hand as Victoria was choking the blood out of my capillaries under the table. Then it happened. *He* happened. Doug let loose with a huge laugh, and when the rest of the family recognized his approval, they followed.

When the table chatter resumed, Doug looked at me and quietly said, "That was ballsy, huh?" I turned back and nodded with the utmost gratitude to him for having my back.

"After you gave that toast," Doug continued, "you helped me see something in a unique way." He admitted that in his adulthood he has come to peace with life being short because of his strong relationship with Christ and his pure love for his wife, Kathy. By devoting himself to his faith and my beautiful mother-in-law, true joy is inspired in Doug. I instantly respected him for not only offering me his unsolicited answers to a difficult question in "why" he is fulfilled in life, but also for being so vulnerable with me right off the bat. As he started to circle back to where he was headed, I realized I had already learned from his example what he was trying to say and just how true it really is. Life is too short to spend in small talk. Yet we all find ourselves engaging in such conversations daily, mostly for selfish motives. I didn't feel I deserved any credit for his brief enlightenment, so I reminded him of what I said in my toast, and we laughed together. Then he turned and raised his glass to the table and told an equally offensive joke that had the table in shambles.

"Who's next?" he asked, and we spent the rest of the dinner going around the table telling inappropriate jokes.

At the time, I didn't think of Doug's act as more than covering my back, but now I see it for what I believe to be his underlying message. Always be true to yourself and be vulnerable with those you love, and joy will follow.

Don't Major in the Minors

Many people these days focus on small issues and miss the big picture. Instead of being distracted with interruptions, even urgent ones, try to do your best to stay focused on your single most important objective until that task is complete.

Another great way to be in the moment during work or in a meeting is to ask why the person presenting does what they do the way they do it. Look for patterns and simple answers in their reply. Always try to further simplify the issues to allow focus on the most important part of the problem. Making the complex understandable requires intense focus. This will allow you to focus on the major issues that are central to solving the problem.

I once asked a senior executive at a massive multi-billion-dollar company with numerous divisions to break down his business into just a few sentences. As a result, I totally understood everything about the business at its core. It was a reply as simple as "We invent technology, manufacture hardware, develop software, and provide services to our customers around the world in order to make their businesses better." Wow! How simple is that? It cuts right to the chase and immediately makes their business understandable.

Try to create simple definitions like this for your own work or responsibilities. Do so by focusing on what really matters most, being in the moment and majoring on the majors. My newly minted son-in-law just informed me that he has written on the white board in his office "Mitchell— are there fewer things you should be doing today with greater focus to make more of an impact?" Try it. Write down the major things you should be focusing on right now!

_____

_____

_____

_____

_____

_____

_____

Faster, Better, Cheaper

Another focus and productivity hack I utilize is with technology and techniques that help me get more done. Ask yourself: *How can I better focus on this right now? How am I being "here" right now?* For example, when I was a partner with another firm, I would get between 20 and 30 voice mails a day. (Back in the old days we used voice mail. In fact, before there was email or the Internet we would call and speak to each other, what a concept.)

But seriously, can you imagine listening to 20-30 voice mails a day? Then consider all the action items that might be required to respond to each message.

After wading through all the information, details, and actions necessary, I developed this trick. I asked people in my message to them to do the following: State your name. Tell me if your message is urgent or if I can listen to it later. Get to the point and tell me what action you need from me. That's it.

People would call me and say, "Hi, Doug. It's so and so. We're having trouble with client X. I need you to do Y."And just from that short message, I would know what I needed to do. I did the same thing with email. It works great, and I believe most people don't read entire emails today anyway, they skim to get to the part that requires a response or action.

That little trick alone saved me countless hours and allowed me to make the best use of my time. What apps or time-management technique can you use to allow you to stay focused and increase your productivity? Said another way, what are you doing to stay focused on the task and not get interrupted by other less important tasks?

Leading Indicators and Outcome Measures

Another way to increase your focus is by following leading indicators and outcome measures. Leading indicators are the two or three things that really move the needle for you, and they generally precede the outcome measure. These are your top priorities. They are the results you are responsible for and what you get paid to accomplish.

Outcome measures are the results of leading indicators. For instance, working out a couple of times a week and eating right are leading indicators—changes made in advance of an outcome. Dropping five pounds over the summer as a result of those changes, is the outcome measure.

Think of it like this. Say a "widget" sales rep wants to make $100,000 a year. And let's assume that they have to sell 54 widgets to meet that financial goal. To sell 54 units, they need 200 qualified prospects. Finding those 200 prospects requires them to market to 600 people by doing things like going to trade shows, attending networking events, and making sales calls. In essence, they first identify their income goal—outcome measure—and then work backwards on their leading indicators to measure their progress along the way. Cold calls and networking are leading indicators. They will "lead" to the outcome of the process, which—in this case—is the desired $100k income.

But add another level to this, and it ties back into my point on focus and productivity. Instead of just playing the numbers—trying to get in front of 600 people as fast as possible—why not take the time and make an extra effort to focus on the top 200 qualified prospects you can present to right away? In other words, find a different approach to achieve the same outcome.

Undoubtedly, doing this kind of focused planning and homework will be much *harder* than trying to market to the masses. But it's also a much *smarter* way to work. You could potentially double or even triple your output with fewer interactions. This type of concentrated and condensed sales cycle will probably also allow you to hit your income goal much faster. But again, you have to focus.

Here's an example from a colleague of mine of what happens when you trust this process.

> Our firm had been working with Doug's company for about 18 months. We had come together with Doug and other colleagues at his organization for an off-site working session. A key focus was to reconcile the wide range of leading indicators for the business—which were strongly moving in the right direction—with the last quarter's revenue and profit performance—which were below expectations.
>
> As we look back, this was a moment that truly tested our beliefs that focusing on the right things, demonstrating persistence in the face of challenges, and trusting the power of leading indicators to further guide your efforts will ultimately pay off.
>
> We catalogued and sharpened the collective story of these leading indicators, continued to execute and

learn, reassured people along the way, and now, two years later, the company is performing at a level never before seen in its history."

Execution Is the Key

A key life lesson for me is that execution is the key. You just have to get it done. Just start. Get to work and take action. Do something today because that's the only way to reach your goals, make progress, and achieve something.

When I hear colleagues say "This is a very big project," I'll ask them "So what's the progress?" And they may come back to me with "Well, we're going to get together again in the next two weeks, and we're going to develop a plan over the next 90 days..." And I'm like "No, no, you can't take that approach. You can't take 90 days to create a plan." You might be able to take 90 days to *complete* the plan, but not *create* it.

Instead, in the first two weeks, you need to figure out where the low hanging fruit is and how you can get some quick wins. That way you build momentum and gain some extra confidence. Ask yourself: *What are the things you can execute on now? Are there things you need to start doing now that might take a long time to develop or could possibly hold the project up?* If so, do those things now so you can get this thing moving and have it all done on time. The lesson is to stop hiding behind your plan and start executing.

It's one of the Principles of Agile Methodology—it's easier to do something in short bursts, then learn and improve as you go. Try to get a working prototype up and running in a month, and then, when you do it again the second month, you will have learned all these lessons that wouldn't have been possible without a prototype.

It goes back to trying new things and reframing failure as a learning event. That way each time you do it, you'll get better and better. So, when you look at a business problem, or a situation in your personal life, don't be like so many people who get lost in the weeds by analyzing all the little itty-bitty parts. That's how things become daunting. Stay focused on the outcome you want to achieve and take focused action.

Focus on What You Can Control

If you're new in your career, in transition, or just the proverbial "low man or woman on the totem pole," you may not be able to control much in your organization. You're probably not signing off on the budget or controlling company mergers. It may seem like there's not much you can control when you're just starting out.

You can control yourself: Your attitude, punctuality, personal actions and results, and how you communicate and interact with your team. So always do your job as best you can. Show up on time and be prepared. Be willing to learn new things. Do your homework and put in the extra hours. Even though those might sound like little things, trust me, they make a big difference.

Recently, an intern gave me a presentation, this person has been with our company about 90 days. They were remarkable, they had taken many of our client-based results, put them in a system that allowed us to review those results within clients, across clients, and across products. This intern spent hours talking to people, studying the data, and creating the system, and his observations were astonishing. I told the intern's manager that I would have a standing offer waiting for this person when they finished college!

Stay focused on those things that you can control and don't worry about the rest. Don't worry if you think your boss is a dork or if they look at you funny. Remind yourself that you're right where God wants you to be, and you're responsible for *you*. If your company gets bought tomorrow, or the CEO decides to fire you, then that's on them. Your job is to do the best you can, day in and day out.

As you narrow your focus onto what really matters, you can make a huge impact in every area of your life. Most people do the complete opposite. They waste time on the trivial *many* instead of focusing on the vital *few*, and ultimately,they have very little impact because of it.

That's why I believe doing fewer things better will always be more beneficial than doing several things with mediocrity. So, what are you focused on today? Are there fewer things you could be doing with greater focus to make more of an impact?

Make two lists: what you should be focused on, and what you need to drop (this will be the harder of the two lists).

_____

_____

_____

_____

_____

_____

Chapter 5

LISTENING TO UNDERSTAND

"Most people do not listen with the intent to understand;
they listen with the intent to reply."
—Stephen R. Covey

"We have but two ears and one mouth
so that we may listen twice as much as we speak."
—Thomas Edison

"Hearing is listening to what is said.
Listening is hearing what isn't said."
—Simon Sinek

Growing up, my dad used to tell me that God gave me two ears and one mouth, and that I was to use them proportionately. Good, active listening is one of the hardest skills to train or master. But listening in order to understand is key to finding real success and meaning in life. To top it off, sometimes asking just one good follow-up question can totally change the trajectory of your life.

Stephen Covey said that people really don't listen to understand, they listen to respond. If you take the time to listen to understand and then follow up with a question instead of a statement, it could change your life as it did mine.

This happened to me years ago when I started dating my wife. We had been working out together for a year, side-by-side on the treadmills at the golf club before we ever went out on a date. Typically, at these kinds of gyms, everybody is married. We both assumed that each of us just wasn't wearing our wedding rings because we didn't like to wear them when we were working out. So, I had no idea she was single. This is an example of me not listening. I was told that on several occasions she showed interest in me, but I was not actively listening. Once I did listen, then it was my turn to ask her the question.

Here we had been working out next to each other, side-by-side, for a whole year. All the while, we enjoyed each other's company without any kind of ulterior motive. Then one day, I finally asked her, "Are you married?" and that's what led to our first date.

Asking the Question Behind the Question

When I say "active" listening, I mean more than just keeping eye contact with the person you're talking to. I mean actually understanding the meaning behind the conversation and demonstrating that you understand.

If someone asks me, "Hey did you get that report done last week?" I'll think about the meaning behind their question. Are they asking me if I got my report done because they didn't receive it? Or because they don't think I've been consistent with turning it in? Or maybe they felt like the report looked bad? What was the question *behind* their question?

I was out at a really nice dinner with some friends recently, and one of them asked the sommelier "What's the most interesting white wine you have?" All of a sudden the sommelier lit up and started asking my friend, "Well tell me more about yourself. Tell me about your palate?" He just started asking all kinds of things like that. Even though that was more of a fun example, it gets to the point of seeking the question *behind* the question. He obviously could tell we enjoyed wine. He made the effort to understand us better in order to serve our specific wants and needs.

When someone's either talking to you or asking you questions, there's always a reason why. Are you clued in enough to actually understand what's really going on in the conversation? Are you aware of what they're asking you about? That's the point of asking the question behind the question.

The Importance of Active Listening

When people are giving presentations in front of the executive leadership team, it's important that the audience actively listens and that the speaker also listens to the audience. It's *crucially* important.

Do you stop to think about what they are saying and why they chose to show the slide they are showing? Active listening will give you a whole different level of involvement than just passively listening to them talk and looking at their slides with a blank stare. They could have put any number of slides in their presentation, so why did they put that slide in there? Ask yourself why it was so important to include that slide?

It's easy to sit back and passively watch life go by, but it's more interesting to choose to listen and understand why things are happening and to learn why people do what they do. By focusing on fewer items, as discussed, you will have time to focus on this presentation and not be worried about making the next meeting.

Think Straight, Talk Straight

This was a slogan we had at one of my previous companies. It helps people cut through all the fat and get to the point. When I give someone a performance review, I always start the evaluation off with what I think about their performance that year.

I'd say, right off the bat, "I think your performance was great this year," or if they had a bad year, "I think your performance was sub-par." That way they know their general performance review within my first sentence. Then I will give them the details, but I don't give them 27 details first, and then tell them how their performance was. That's just too confusing and drawn out. Yet, that's exactly how executives run their employees' performance reviews each year.

It's been like that with bosses I've had in the past. When my boss was an outward processor and a really verbal communicator, he would typically spout out four or five things about me that were very negative. But then he would kind of self-correct and feel bad that he was being so negative. Then we could finally get into what mattered and truly have a much more meaningful conversation.

I came to learn that those first four or five negative things he would say to me were really just his way of clearing out things he may have been baffled by, or what he was worried about. While it is important to deal with those areas, that may not be the right moment. He was really just that kind of an unfiltered guy. So I had to ask him the question *behind* the questions to really learn his communication style. Then, I didn't take it personally.

Listening for Insight

Listening to gain insight is, for me, one of the higher forms of listening. It's where you get past all the physical capabilities of actively listening and put yourself in the situation to hear what's really being said—and *not* being said. It means being interested *in* others rather than just trying to be interesting *to* them.

Listening for insight is the type of "deep" listening you do when you really sit back and watch *how* people communicate, and hear *what* they are communicating. I think it gives you deeper insight into their motivation. Once you really understand a person's motivation, then you can unlock their potential. You can begin to coach them and help them improve. But if I can't get to the motivating reasons behind the "why" you're doing something or how you're doing it, then I'm just being superficial in the whole relationship.

I want to share a story from a client and friend who is a corporate coach, author, and speaker of truth. She has helped me in my career over the last six years, and she is the main reason I decided to write this book.

> In multiple business interactions with Doug over several years, what has struck me most is what a thoroughly decent human being he is. Doug is the real deal. He genuinely lives and practices what he preaches. The reason I enjoy working with him— which results in much more productive business results—is that Doug listens. He listens, not only

with his ears, but with his eyes, his head, and his heart.

Let me share a recent example. One spring, I had been going nonstop and was close to physical exhaustion. Doug and I were working together during a particularly hectic—and fruitful—strategic planning session that I was facilitating. I asked the group of senior leaders in the room (which included Doug) if anyone was good at flip chart scribing. No one jumped up to grab the marker, so I continued. When we broke for lunch, my writing arm started hurting quite severely. (It turned out later that I had torn a rotator cuff and didn't know it.)

The session resumed after lunch, and by then I was holding up my right arm with my left, as it became increasingly uncomfortable to write on the flip chart. Suddenly, out of the corner of my eye, I saw movement. Out of all the leaders present, Doug—and only Doug—had noticed my discomfort. He had listened to my question before lunch and asked himself—*why has she, for the first time in so many sessions, asked if any of us can scribe well?* Putting two and two together, he tactfully moved forward to assist me. Quietly taking the marker out of my hand, he said casually, "Why don't you facilitate while I scribe? Though my writing won't be as good as yours!"

I handed him the marker with gratitude. That's the kind of leader I want to follow, to learn from, to be around. Needless to say, regardless of my schedule, if there is anything I can help Doug with—I'll do it.

That, in my opinion, is an example of practicing what you preach. I would recommend you read the chapter around the power of listening especially carefully. It has powerful insights into the tools that help leaders lead from both the head and the heart.

Understanding Mental Models

Everybody has their own frames of reference for how they think life should go. I call these frames of reference a person's mental model. I believe everybody walks into situations with specific thoughts, beliefs, and opinions about how they think things are. Those thoughts, those mental models, shape that person's reality and how they listen.

Maybe they were teased as a kid, and therefore, they feel that they have to present themselves as strong and emotionally impenetrable. Maybe they had a parent who rode them hard when they failed at something. Now they strive for perfection. Whatever it is, there are certain things that affect us as we're growing up, and, in turn, influence how we perceive the world and respond to things as adults.

Maybe your mental model regarding political parties is that all Republicans eat their children, or you believe that all Democrats only want to tax the rich and give government unlimited oversight. Or maybe you think organized religion is evil, or you have strong opinions about social issues. Whatever it is, just realize that you have these belief patterns, these mental models, and they shape your thinking and behavior.

Exposing these mental models, my own included, helps us to understand each other better. It helps us understand why we have certain visceral reactions to ideas, situations, or other things. It is also why some issues just resonate with us at a heart level. It's not that these models are right or wrong, necessarily, they're just our reality.

I have dealt with many mental models—race, gender, age, background, education etc. If you know your mental model, you can expose it to help you, or you can use it to dismiss others. One of my favorite stories was when I was at Arthur Andersen. We were sitting in a large classroom discussing mental models and how the brain uses these models to process information for our benefit. The instructor gave this example. He was parked at a shopping mall where he had driven his wife to do some shopping. He wanted to sit in the car and think (well, he is a Harvard professor!). He said it started to rain and at first the raindrops were just that, drops on the windshield all separated and unique. Then, as the rain started to intensify, the drops started to pool and run in channels down the window. They were no longer individual raindrops they were now channels of water. He explained that that is how your brain functions. When someone yells "fire," you run out of the building, you don't hang around and discuss it, you move into action.

In the same way our brain makes us efficient by channeling similar words or thoughts into channels, you have a mental model to process thoughts, which, in the fire's case, is good but in business may be bad. You need to see the individual drops and understand them in order to get the most out of it. As you start to channel your next conversation, understand you are no longer listening for understanding, you are channeling and missing the drops.

Shifting the mental models of employees doesn't just happen because the boss snaps his or her fingers and orders a shift. You have to get people to believe they are capable of something they currently don't think they can do. Here is an actual testimonial from a client of mine about how it worked in their company.

> The following is a story that I think best demonstrates Doug's ability to question his mental models, see an opportunity when no one else could, and mobilize thousands of people to believe in something that just 100 days before they thought virtually impossible.

> Several years ago while working with Doug, we were at a crossroads with a failing business unit. What should we do? Sell it? Lay off most of the workforce to cut costs to the bone? Let it putter out over time and squeeze as much money from it as possible?

When looking at most of the logical data points, a normal person would categorize this as a classic "falling knife" situation—you never want to be the person who ends up having to catch it. But Doug went deeper to better understand the larger market and what this business had to offer. When the opportunity arose to take responsibility for turning the business around, Doug volunteered. I was there when he raised his hand, and I can tell you there were relieved sighs filling the room.

Where others saw failure and the possible loss of their jobs, Doug saw opportunity and growth. Doug had pushed his mental models and now saw an opportunity he was willing to risk his job for, but the challenge now was how to scale this mental model when everyone in the business unit had, for years, held the mental model that they were a failing business unit—a perception the company's executives had reinforced time and again!

In just 90 days, I watched as Doug turned this business unit around in such a compelling, effective, and fun manner that he created a sense of FOMO across the larger enterprise. People from every area of the company—mind you, people who seemingly had no skin in the game with the success or failure of this business unit—were *volunteering* their discretionary time to help catch this "falling knife." So what did Doug do so differently? He invested the time needed to build a focused and aligned sense of urgency around a new mental model that would drive dramatically better results. In just 90 days, the trajectory of the business unit was unstoppable. They were about to go on a run that, for many, would be a highlight of their careers.

What are some of your mental models, perceptions?

_____

_____

_____

_____

_____

_____

_____

CHAPTER 6:

LEARN MORE TO EARN MORE

"The more you learn, the more you earn."
—WARREN BUFFETT

"Never stop learning because life never stops teaching."
—ANONYMOUS

"Be humble, be coachable, and always keep learning."
—ANONYMOUS

When I was in the third grade, I was asked to play on a basketball team. Back then, sports were very different from how they are today. It was more just a dad gathering a few kids from the neighborhood and then other parents would kind of help out by supporting the school's program. But growing up, I was the kid who was always in trouble. I was the class clown and was always behind in my homework. Before school, I used to watch the older kids play pickup games out in the yard. It was so awesome that many kids would come early to watch these guys play basketball. I wanted to be one of them when I "grew up." But like I said, I was always in trouble.

Well, one day, this neighborhood dad who had watched me try to play with his sons came to my front door to ask my parents if I could play on his basketball team. I think it was because I was very tall as a youngster. My mom answered the door and told him "no" because I had been in trouble. He stopped my mom right there and said:

> "You know, that's a good approach to discipline, but with some of my boys I have used a different technique. Could I offer you an alternative solution? Why don't you let Doug come play today, and if he doesn't get caught up on his homework by the end of the week, then he can't come play with us on Saturday when we have a game. But if he keeps his homework up, then he gets to play. How about that?"

My mother was thrilled, first to have a man come to the door to help this troubled kid, but second, because maybe this would work, and her kid would be less of a problem. (You would have to ask my mother how this ultimately worked out!) That was on a Tuesday. I promised my mom I'd get my homework done, and she let me go to basketball practice that afternoon. I loved it.

That neighborhood dad was a very tough coach and really busted our butts. He wanted us to be in shape. Our coach believed that the harder you practiced the better you played, so he pushed us to practice as hard as possible.

The amount of effort we gave was directly related to the playing time we received.

We also learned a lot from college coaches. Our favorite at the time was John Wooden from UCLA, and many of our drills were fashioned after the ones his teams ran. Our drills were all about being a team, fast breaks with the ball never touching the floor, and many others that made us depend on each other. The first part of the practice consisted of conditioning drills as he believed the deeper into the game, the team in the better shape would have an advantage. Kids who had great individual skills but not a team interest were quickly discouraged from coming back until they developed more of a team focus. I had a lot of fun.

Perfect Practice Makes Perfect Performance

In order to get better and put in more practice, I asked my dad to put up a basketball hoop over our garage. I'd be out there practicing for hours after school. For me, the concept of "perfect practice makes perfect performance" has stuck. I remember shooting free throws for instance. I would shoot 100 free throws in a row. Then I'd shoot 20 bounce shots, and then I'd shoot another 100 free throws.

The whole idea of shooting a free throw the same way over and over again was so helpful. I would practice using my wrist the same way every time, so that when game time came, and I got fouled, I could confidently shoot a free throw even if I was tired. I had already shot thousands of free throws in practice, so it became very easy for me. I excelled because I spent the extra time learning how to shoot free throws and practicing other skills.

I went from fourth grade all the way through eighth grade playing on that basketball team. Our team played in Hawaii, Las Vegas, Oregon, and Kentucky, and in so many local tournaments, it's hard to count. Just think about that. Here we were, a bunch of sixth, seventh, and eighth graders, out traveling because we could not find any basketball teams in the neighborhood who could give us a good game. All of us were literally from the same elementary school, but we were good because we learned how to practice.

How you practice is how you're going to play. It's true for sports, and it's true for life. And whether you're learning a foreign language or how to give a speech or facilitate a meeting, it's all the same: Perfect practice makes perfect performance. It all comes down to practicing that skill over and over. If you want to get good, you'll need to practice.

Learning to Hack My Way to Disneyland

My degree is in computer science, and one of the things I love about it is that everything we do can be considered practice, it's never really done. So, I practiced writing programs, all kinds of programs, diagnostics, and test routines. In college, I wrote a program that emulated a user log-in screen so that users would log into my screen thinking they were on the actual computer screen, and I could take their passwords, write sayings back to them, and generally fake them out. It was fun to watch the business students so confused, not knowing what was going on. Picture this: you're a college student—back in the 80s—typing into the mainframe at your school. You enter your name and password, and all of a sudden, the computer responds: *Dave, I can't believe you are here so early before your project is due!*

It was an unsophisticated form of hacking—the oldest trick in the computer book—but back in the early 1980s, people didn't use computers like we do today. Sure, computers were around, but you had to go to a computer room or computer lab to use them. There weren't laptops and tablets like we have now. In my classes, we got to build different pieces of the actual computer system. We built parts of the operating system that make the user interface connect with the hardware.

Right out of college I was one of the first college graduates hired by Tandem Computers, which was the backbone of a funds transfer network connected to Diebold ATM machines (cash machines). My first job out of college was to write interfaces for other computers that connected to the Tandem network—in this example it was for moving funds around. This enabled the sales team to use Tandem computers in more applications—banking, retail, funds, manufacturing, and process control—to sell more machines.

One of the most interesting projects I worked on was at Disneyland in California. I had to not only program the Tandem computer that was controlling turnstiles, but also the turnstile computer that was actually a process control computer. As the turnstile clicks, there's a computer inside of it counting the clicks. I programmed both computer languages to get the computers to talk to each other so that every thirtieth guest would win a prize.

What was so fun about that was I had to learn how to make the Tandem system perform differently from what it was designed to do—being a stack-based machine vs. a register-based machine—that's another story! I had to learn how to get the other computer system to drive an outcome that the entertainment park wanted. This type of work was fascinating. When it worked, I felt masterful.

This was when Disneyland was experiencing a down-turn in people walking through the turnstiles. My under-standing is that with the Disneyland business model, everything they sell inside the park pays all the overhead, and everybody who walks through the turnstiles is profit.

Disneyland needed more people coming through the turnstiles. They devised this plan: every thirtieth guest would win a prize. It could be anything from a $50 gift coupon to a new car. Whatever it was, I had to program the computer to count the clicks on the turnstile, then I had to get a random number generator and print a ticket so that by the time the person walked through the turnstile, the ticket would print on the other side and show them if they had won a prize.

If you think about it like a subway, you know how you scan your card, and the turnstile opens. Well at Disneyland, it was the other way around. You would walk through the turnstile, and then print a ticket out on the other end of the turnstile. When you walked through it, you pulled the ticket out on the other side. That's how fast it had to be. It had to be able to process 18 guests a second.

Adventures in Programming

All of that helped me launch my career because I enjoyed learning more about computers and programming. I learned all about these other computer systems. One time I had to interface with a computer that moved 100-thousand-pound devices to pour molten aluminum. I worked on another computer for the B-1 bomber that had to learn a robotic system that dispatched robotic trays on rollers out to technicians working on the airplanes.

I enjoyed learning all this new stuff. Here I was putting myself out there, and I was this young new computer engineer, clearly not as qualified as the older engineers. The difference was they didn't want to learn all this new technology, and I did. They didn't want to have to deal with the other computers that they didn't know anything about, and they sure didn't want to have to deal with all the challenges that making computers talk to one another can create.

Because I was curious and wanted to learn, I got the fun opportunities. I would learn and then practice, then learn and practice some more. I encourage you to try new things as well. Because you never know what kind of opportunities you will get as a result.

I wasn't learning it to become a better programmer, I was learning it to become a better businessperson and problem solver. The tools in my toolbox happened to be that I knew how to program. Later, I would learn how to write software, and even more opportunities opened up. You should take every chance you get to learn and practice new skills, because they really can help you down the road.

Learning How to Sell

After I learned about programming systems, the company moved me into writing some software and teaching engineers how to use it. Ultimately, I moved into working with clients who wanted to learn to use our technology. I was now a sales engineer. The idea was that as the sales engineer, I would go out and use these computers that were worth millions of dollars to help companies solve their problems. Here I was, at 28 or 29 years old, talking to clients about how to use these million-dollar technologies back in the mid-1980s.

Here I was, again, doing something I really didn't know anything about—sales! I had never sold anything in my life, but I was doing it because I was willing to learn. That's when I started to pick up the Ziglar books and learned about prospecting, cold calling, blanketing, and filling my pipeline.

I would read these books to learn the art of selling. I learned consultative selling, and how to ask questions. I learned how to understand what the client's needs are, because—at the end of the day—nobody likes to be sold, but everybody likes to buy. Remember that phrase, it will help you in the long run!

I moved up in my career because of selling, and I was successful. Later when I moved to a global technology company, I was involved with a very large consulting project where I was on a team that created a billion-dollar deal. My rags-to-riches story was made possible by practicing the skill of selling and learning how to solve people's problems.

The Importance of Team Learning

There are two aspects of learning: personal learning and team learning. Personal learning is what I've been talking about—learning new skills because you're curious or passionate about something. Team learning is learning with others and figuring out your role on the team. That's a big area of learning that people tend to overlook. They assume they can play the same role on every team, but that's rarely the case. Excellent players can be fluid in their roles and adjust as needed to the left or to the right.

During parts of my career, I have had to work directly with five to twelve direct reports—all of them successful people—day in and day out, in essence a team. As company goals are established and the team's focus are aligned, one of the things I continue to fight against is that a few have the mentality of a zero-sum game. These few think that if they help the company goal, it may deter them from their individual goal. They act like they're only going to help others if it helps them, or if they are sure to get credit. Life is not a zero-sum game. Help others be successful, and your career will take off.

I've had to continually coach on team learning. I usually make a basketball analogy. I'll say:

> "You know, what's great about us as a team is that every single one of us wants to be the best individual contributor. It's natural for players to want to have the most baskets, the most rebounds, and the most assists. But if we play like individuals, then as a team, we may lose the game."

I'll ask them, "Is it your individual performance that's lacking? Or is it your team performance that's lacking?"

When you're on a team, it's the team—not any one player—that's most important. And so really giving up your own selfish desires and ego is what's needed to make sure the team wins. I have seen this quote hanging over the door to many gym locker rooms: "There Is No 'I' in Team!" This should be hanging in more business conference rooms!

It's important to have everyone on the team decide that winning together is better than winning alone. It will also be the most rewarding, both monetarily and personally. The skills that you learn and build as a team will always be a lot more fun than building individual skills.

Here's a story from one of my colleagues regarding teamwork.

> In corporate America, all too often, leaders are obsessed with efficiency versus effectiveness. This means numbers, numbers, and still more numbers. As an engineer I am completely aware of the numbers, but I learned mid-career that high performing teams need much more than individual targets and goals. Self-awareness, interpersonal skills, and an overall high emotional intelligence are all critical towards achieving team and organizational outcomes.
>
> A few years ago, Doug and I were working together on a mission critical project for the organization. Though the multi-functional group assigned to this project was made up of highly successful and talented individuals, they were struggling through the "storming and forming" phases, and their interactions with each other were siloed and sometimes acrimonious. The output was, understandably, suboptimal. Doug, as the senior leader leading this charge, recognized the importance of building a high performing team. He references this multiple times in this book when he talks about individual versus team performance.

Doug encouraged the group to look inside, to build self-awareness, to examine not just how, but *why*, they function in silos. He personally sponsored a session aimed at building a high EQ, high performing team. He kicked off the session by opening up about his past missteps. He told us he had learned to move towards a team-focused approach for better business outcomes. He was open, he was vulnerable, he was humble. As a result of Doug's sponsorship of this initiative, team members started looking deeply into their own emotional intelligence and communication styles. A dialog was opened about how being a blunt "hammer" during communications may hurt others in the group. We learned how to listen more generously and how to develop joint team goals. It became safe to be real, it became safe to give and receive feedback, and it became safe to question impractical processes, timeliness, and tasks. And together, meaningful, difficult, yet reachable goals were agreed upon.

Two years later, I am happy to say this team has had extraordinary results and outcomes. The process improvements they have initiated have helped improve both revenue and morale. This is a cohesive, "high fun, high functioning" team now. And, along the way, under Doug's strong and inclusive guidance, they have learned to shift for positive change.

CHAPTER 7:

TEACH WHAT YOU KNOW

"Teaching is the act of sharing the knowledge we have been given by others with the hope that someday, in some way, it again will be passed on."
—ANONYMOUS

"People learn the most when teaching others."
—PETER F. DRUCKER

"If you get, give. If you learn, teach."
—MAYA ANGELOU

I love flying. There are few things I'd rather do than fly. Well maybe sail a catamaran in the British Virgin Islands, but that is a different story. Back when I went to flight school, you had to have about 40 hours of flight time to get your private pilot's license. And you had to have about 20 hours with an instructor in order to fly solo. Once you started to fly solo, you could get the other 20 hours of flying and book testing quickly in order to complete your training.

Included in some of this normal instruction was the use of a simulator. This cut down the cost of utilizing an airplane, was easier to schedule, and it was independent of weather. However, in all my training, I never used a simulator. All of my 40-hour fly-time was flying in the air. I wanted to learn in the real cockpit. My teachers appreciated that because they knew I'd get a much better education by learning in the air and having them teach me in the actual cockpit under real world conditions. To top it off, I was living in Colorado and had to learn how to fly in high altitude. So here I was up at 5000 to 9000 feet flying in the clouds (not literally, that would be against the rules). Throughout this whole process, I would do anything for flight time.

After that, I went on to get my instrument license, which is where the story gets interesting. To get my instrument rating, I needed to have 200 hours of flying time. Think about this, I was a young college kid having to get 200 hours and pay for the cost of all of that rental time, instructor time, books, and testing. Believe me, it's expensive.

I really wanted to earn the 200 hours so I could get my instrument rating. Having that designation would allow me to fly in the winter and at other times that don't qualify under visual flight rules— like when it was foggy out— rather than only being allowed to fly on clear days with a private pilot's license.

I went to school in Northern California, and since I had my pilot's license, I racked up a lot of hours toward my 200 by flying down to Southern California. I would take everybody down for the holidays, then I'd fly everybody back. Or I'd fly friends to Reno, San Francisco, and other fun places we all wanted to visit. Everyone would chip in for expenses on the airplane, and I was earning my flight hours.

Once I had enough time, the FBO[1] would let me ferry a plane from point A to point B and deliver them to the different owners. I did everything I could to fly and get my 200 hours.

I found that the best way to learn was to fly in real time and in real conditions. When I finally went up for my instrument rating, I got an extremely high score—both on the written exam and on the flying test. The instructor asked me, "How much time do you have under the hood?" And I said, "Well, I didn't do any flying that wasn't in instrument conditions. I did all my flying in the clouds." So being in the clouds for my check ride was natural, because that's how I trained. That was how I began teaching others. Whenever I had passengers in the cockpit with me, I would teach them about how all the gadgets and levers worked. The more comfortable I got at teaching others, the more comfortable I was in understanding it myself. When friends asked me questions about how things worked, I had to go and find the answer. This process deepened my knowledge.

---

1   Fixed Base Operator is an organization allowed to operate at airports with various airplane related tasks.

Teaching to Fully Understand

That's why I think that teaching is a wonderful way to give back. Everybody should look for opportunities to teach whatever they know or are passionate about. It doesn't have to be a formal arrangement or anything special. It can be in a casual or informal setting also.

> **You can teach someone through one-on-one mentoring. Or it can even be through peer-to-peer coaching. There are different forms, but teaching is about helping people get better at their own skills and imparting valuable skills that you have to others.**

Teaching makes people more open to learning. Just like my story of learning how to fly in the cockpit of the airplane in real time. I learned in the clouds. I find that those people who are good students tend to be good teachers as well and vice versa.

The whole point of learning and teaching is to really understand what's going on behind the scenes and to see it happen in real time. It's always much easier to teach something in which you have a lot of experience. I feel that because of your experience in something, you can do a much better job of preparing to teach it. Also, you know what it's like to have been a new student, so you know what it takes to learn it.

Here's another example. For a portion of my career, I lived part time in Puerto Rico. Many Puerto Ricans speak mostly Spanish, so I wanted to learn Spanish while I was working on the island. What I found is that learning from people who grew up in Puerto Rico and had spoken the language since birth was harder than learning from someone who had picked up the language later. The later learners understand how difficult it can be. They often have discovered tricks, ways they learned, that you could use too. One great tip for learning another language is to watch TV in that language with subtitles in the same language to see what they are saying. Money!

When you are teaching your subject, you can tell personal stories from your own learning experiences. Stories make the lessons more memorable.

Teaching to Help Others

Teaching is something that everybody should try. Whether you teach your subordinates or a night class on a hobby or volunteer at Sunday school—put yourself out there and do it.

Teaching also helps you learn a subject much better. For instance, if I were going to teach a Sunday school class, like I did years ago, I would really have to begin to look at the Scriptures differently. I'd have to think about the questions someone might have, and I would need to understand the different nuances of the Scripture. Then I'd have to grab two or three different references to that

Scripture to get different people's opinions on what that verse or passage meant. My preparation would be different when I'm teaching than if I were reading the Scriptures on my own.

That's what I want to get across—that the act of teaching will make you better at many other life skills as well, like study, discipline, and the organization of your ideas. You'll also get better at communicating those ideas.

The teaching relationship doesn't have to be a formal one. You don't have to act like a professor. You could teach your peers at the office or coach a co-worker new skills.

You probably have many overlooked skills that are highly valued by others. You might be gifted in technology, math, or at giving live presentations. Whatever it is, teach those skills to others.

> Our consulting firm had been fortunate to be partnering with Doug's company for a couple of years. In our work together, it became clear that, across his career, he had had extraordinary experiences growing companies, specifically in the context of advisory services and consulting.
>
> We asked if he would be open to coming to our headquarters and leading a working session focused on blending his experience with us as a firm, with his vast experience in driving growth, with an emphasis on selling.

This truly was an opportunity for him to teach in a way that helped us understand ourselves as a firm in new ways, pushed our edges around what we could try, gave us new mental models to think about what we do, and most importantly, further built our confidence in the difference we can make with companies and in the world.

To this day, we look back and reference specific advice and ideas that Doug shared, quoting him and leveraging those lessons to help us bring even more "swagger" to our conversations with current and prospective clients. That day created a shift in our firm that has continued to guide us on a trajectory of growth and compounding momentum.

The Importance of Realizing How Others Learn

Teaching is about imparting your knowledge to another individual. To teach someone effectively, you need to realize that different people learn in different ways. Everyone has their own learning style. Maybe they're visual learners, or they prefer interaction, or they are auditory learners. Having to teach something helps you consider taking different approaches into account as opposed to only presenting your material in one, static way. For most of us, it's how we learn. Think about this for a second: how do you teach, how do you like to learn? Are they similar?

Dialogue vs. Discussion

Teaching is also more of a dialogue, whereas the typical business presentation might be considered more of a monologue. There's more interaction and engagement in a teaching situation than there is in a traditional sales presentation.

This is the difference between a dialogue and a discussion. In the consulting world, a big deal is made of the importance of having a "discussion"—which kind of rhymes with percussion. And really, it's a joke because all a discussion is, is me telling you, then you telling me, then me telling you, followed by you telling me...back and forth, back and forth. Both sides are advocating for their cause or position when they're talking, but neither one is really listening to the other, they are formulating the next response. That is how most business meetings go. It seems like this is business as usual in the United States today.

A "dialogue" on the other hand, is a different learning process. It's when participants ask each other questions and really listen to the responses. As a result, the conversation happens at a very different pace. It's slower, because I may not talk for five minutes. And when you're talking, I'm not rushing to mentally form my response. I'm listening and saying, "Oh wow, that's fascinating. Hmmm, that's interesting." Or, "I'd like to know a little bit more about this or that." There's an intentionality on listening and learning in a dialogue.

Be Flexible

Another one of my tips for teaching is to remain flexible. Sometimes it may be easier for you to adapt to your "student" than it is for them to adapt to you. Unfortunately, many of the leaders I know are the complete opposite. They expect the student to bend to them. I always try to teach and coach people based on where they are, not where I am.

If they choose to change because they see the benefit of changing, that's great. I don't want to try to force them if they're not ready to learn. Remember, when you're teaching and coaching others, it's because you're trying to improve their performance or the performance of your team. It can be easier to coach where they are today than it is to try to change them to be more like you want them to be tomorrow.

If you have a team member who's not very attentive to detail, and his job requires some attention to detail, you might suggest that he partner with someone to help him in that area. You might coach him in a way that he realizes that's not his strong suit. Then you can coach him so that he learns to compensate for that lack of skill. By the way, I'm one of those guys. I don't have great attention to detail, so I surround myself with detail-oriented people who can catch things I may miss.

Seek to Help

When you're teaching someone, you need to show them that you are a learner too, and you want to help them out.

It's kind of like me saying; "Oh I'll be nice to my wife when she's nice to me." It's just never going to work out that way. I have to go first and "be nice" to her before I expect it in return.

Being flexible with someone when you are teaching is all about helping them where they are today, rather than trying to get them to change to the way that you want them to be before they're ready for it.

Try this today at your office, home, church, or school. Teach someone, and it will open your eyes to how much better it makes both of you.

How to Teach Your Boss

Coaching "up" can be a delicate matter, but it can have a profound influence on your career if you are patient, flexible, and insightful. Here are some quick tips to help you coach your boss. I have used this in my career to help both of us to be more effective. However, to do it successfully, you need to come from a place of honesty. You also need to have the right amount of confidence, without arrogance. Lastly, seek permission and feedback along the way.

It's really all about your desire to try to help your boss become a better leader, not simply an attempt to stroke your ego or further your own spot in life. The best way to start when you are coaching up is to give your supervisor a few things to do that will really help your team—and, by extension, him—succeed.

I wanted to make sure that my bosses understood the reason I was trying to give them feedback. I hope the same advice holds true for you. Be sure to gain permission from your superiors before you actually start coaching them. And in return, allow them to coach you up, solicit their feedback, and offer up self-analysis to help them gauge how thick your skin is.

An example might be that you go to your boss after a big meeting and say, "I heard your speech to the troops. Do you mind if I give you some feedback." If they are open to it then you can proceed, perhaps lightly.

It's important to see how they respond both verbally and with body language. They may be saying "Yes" with their mouth, but their crossed arms are clearly telling you "No." The bottom line is, you want people to hear what you're telling them because you want to be helpful. The *way* you tell them matters. I always start with the positives. Not only does this allow them to relax, but it really builds confidence. Then you can get into the points to help them, not have them do it your way or manipulate them but to help them. And the next time they give the same kind of talk, they will hear your voice in the back of their head. Make sure you compliment them on what they do well, the higher one goes, the less feedback one gets. As they say, "It's lonely at the top." I would value your feedback!

When is the last time you offered feedback to someone? How did it go? What would you do differently next time?

CHAPTER 8

HOW TO ASK BETTER QUESTIONS

"The art and science of asking questions
is the source of all knowledge."
—THOMAS BERGER

"The important thing is not to stop questioning."
—ALBERT EINSTEIN

"I never learn anything talking.
I only learn things when I ask questions."
—LOU HOLTZ

M y father used to always tell me, "You're defined by the questions you ask." And there is a famous quote by Abraham Lincoln that says, "Better to remain silent and be thought a fool than to speak and to remove all doubt." That quote, along with my father's advice, has always stayed in the back of my head when I ask a question.

Then, there are people in business today who say, "There's no such thing as a dumb question." I think that's total crap too. So, which is it? Are you defined by the questions you ask? Or is there no such thing as a dumb question?

I would say that the former is truer than the latter. Today you are defined by the questions you ask. For example, have you ever been in a meeting or had a conversation with someone, and you are on step five, and they ask you about step one? What does that say about them? Do you wonder if they are able to keep up? Do they even understand what it is you're talking about? Was it a dumb question? Yes, there are dumb questions. Now maybe it was a good question for them as they are not keeping up, but is that how you want to be remembered. Questions are often better asked offline or in a smaller group.

I'll give you another example, have you ever gone into a room and asked a question, and everybody stops and just looks at you? And that is then followed by a long pause? Sure, it could be that you asked a good, thought-provoking question. But nine times out of ten, it's because you asked a dumb question, or the material was already covered, and you missed it. They're all looking at you with a blank stare, wondering, "Where the heck did that come from?"

How Not to Ask

Part of learning how to ask good questions is learning how not to ask dumb ones. One of the worst things you could do is to ask a question that you already know the answer to just so you can show off your special knowledge or insight. How many people have you seen in a meeting who have asked a leading question, because they're dying to answer it themselves? All this shows is their insecurity and their need to be heard and understood. Maybe they need validation of why they're at the meeting. My advice is: if you're in the meeting, *you're in the meeting*. If you don't know why you're there, fake it till you make it. Instead, ask a question to better understand.

Another thing to really think about is asking a question from a different level than that of the conversation. I use a macro vs. micro description for this. Some people like to focus on the micro issues, when really it may be the macro ones that matter most, or vice versa.

Make sure that you're staying on par with the conversation—unless there's a scope to go deeper—and ask a micro question that's relevant. If you're talking about the overall budget of the company, division by division, don't ask about one of the cost items three ledgers down under a sub-ledger—that's not what the conversation is about. Even if you're trying to show off your awareness, or document your capabilities, because you know the details buried down a bit lower, you're changing the level of the conversation. You need to be conscious of the level of conversation that you're having.

Another tip for not asking bad questions is to not make a statement as part of your question. I've been in many public forums — conferences and presentations — where somebody will walk to the microphone, and after introducing themselves, launch into a two-and-a-half minute statement. This often causes the person presenting to respond, "Is there a question in that?" There are certain circumstances that demand this type of response. What we are working on here is the art of asking a good question. Practice it.

The Right Way to Ask Questions

If you frame it up the right way, then there really is no dumb question. I know that may sound contradictory to what I said earlier, but if you truly don't understand something and you ask the question, even if it is a simple question, it will still define who you are. If you ask a simple question, it doesn't mean it's necessarily a bad question. It just means that you don't fully understand what's been said or done. Some people use this technique to demonstrate an obvious answer. I would just offer the obvious answer and skip the object lesson of the question. A big part of this is being conscious of your audience. It may be easier, and less embarrassing, to ask somebody else to catch you up later than to ask a question in a large group setting.

Another way to ask questions is to be genuinely curious about the topic. When you are authentic in your curiosity, people will see that you are really trying to learn. As such, they will be less quick to judge your motivations.

Another tip would be: don't try to understand too fast. For instance, there are a lot of people who want to show off how smart they are and how they learn very quickly. So they go "Yeah, yeah, I got that. Yeah, yeah, I got that." To me, that's confirmation that they get it, and we're moving on to the next topic. If this is true, great, if it's not true, don't fall into this trap. Try to use the information in an example in your head to fully understand the concept.

One of the things that I did while consulting was to say, "We are going to take a word that everybody understands— let's use the word 'physician' for example. I want you to write down five meanings of what the word 'physician' means."

We were in a room of fifteen people, and we all wrote down the word *physician*, along with five meanings. Do you know how many words we had that day in common? Or definitions that everybody agreed on? None.

To me, "not understanding too fast" means really listening to the comments and asking good questions and making sure you are getting to the core issue that you need to understand. That may mean asking a second question or a third question as a follow-up. Listening, as was discussed in an earlier chapter, is an art and very hard to master.

Asking follow up questions will allow you to go deeper and understand what it is that the individual is trying to communicate to you. Secondly, it allows them to elaborate. When you ask a person a second or third question, they will tend to take a little longer with their answer. They may go a little bit slower, and they may add a little more detail. You end up getting a more complete answer. This helps to get deeper in understanding.

Promotion by Questioning

Once, we were performing a service for an extremely large client. I was in charge of markets for our company, which really means sales and account management for the organization. Unfortunately, we were watching our results for this one particular client go down and down.

We were trying to understand what was going on. I wasn't concerned with the operational teams—the people delivering the product—neither was I involved with the people ingesting the data, I was just in charge of the account management and sales team.

I asked the question, "Why is it going down and down?" I got one explanation from the operations team and another from fulfillment, and I kept getting the run around from everyone. But I continued to ask questions. I went to my boss and my co-boss and told them, "These people just aren't really responding. They're not really getting it done. My client is still very, very unhappy."

Due to my tenaciousness and curiosity which led me to ask questions, I earned a reputation for myself. One day, my boss came in and said, "The leader of that other group, basically said, 'I'm tired of coming in here and asking all these questions.' I need a leader who can ask questions. I want you to go run this."

That's what started my promotion from being the president of markets to being president of markets *and* running about a third of the company's operations.

This curiosity has helped my career as I've continued to ask questions and dive deeper into the business. Eventually, I was promoted to Chief Operations Officer, overseeing operations, sales, and account management. Curiosity and questions played a large part in my promotion as the company started to perform better and work more as a team continuing to focus on the client.

Years ago, I was asked to run one division; because I asked questions, I now run the two largest divisions. I spend time trying to understand others. I am willing to ask questions, and my goal is to help other people. These added responsibilities were not due to my superior intellect, working all hours of day and night, or threatening everyone within an inch of their careers. I just knew we, as a team, could perform better, and I wanted to find out how to unleash the power of these teams.

Look Into the Meaning, More Than the Answer

Looking into meaning more than the answer is about knowing what someone is really saying when they answer your question. It's the message behind the words they say. It's the meaning behind their response. It's also what their body language is conveying, what their facial expressions are, and how their intonation changes.

Looking for the meaning is about asking "What are they communicating to me beyond just the words that are coming out of their mouth?" If I ask a good question, then the answer I get back will give me a lot of helpful information—both tactically and semantically.

Head and Heart Questions

I always feel that, in business, we miss the hard questions, and these tend to be the *heart* questions. One of those questions is, "How do you feel about that?" When someone says, "You know, I really want to do this" or "I really want to do that." Often, we don't ask them, "Well, how do you feel about that?"

Once when my team was working on a proposal, a team member was going through the pricing and margin analysis and competition. I said, "How did you come up with the price you came up with?" And he said, "Well, to meet our corporate margin requirements, that's our price."

So, I asked, "How do you feel about that?" (You know, what I wanted to say? "What an idiot. Why would you price something because of corporate margin requirements? Maybe because if you lose the deal, then you get to pass blame and say, *'Well, the company priced it wrong.'"*)

Well?

So I asked him, "Well, how did you feel about the pricing?" He said that he didn't feel it was very competitive. So I said, "Do you really want us to approve pricing that's not competitive?" To which he replied, "Well, no." So I said, "Well, then—what? Where should our pricing land to be competitive?" He gave us another range of numbers.

Then I asked, "Why is that new number competitive versus the other number?" He went through the data. I said, "When you think about how we priced it last time on this contract, you know what happened." He then went through additional historical information on pricing, back to all the technical scoring, the detailed pricing scores, and how much bidding we did and how different our price was versus our next competitor. Then he explained how our technical score was versus our next competitor. And we had a lot of really good data on why it should be this other number.

I looked at our CFO, and said, "I think that's the right number. I think we should bet on that view." Then I asked the team, "How does everybody feel about taking less margin and doing the right number for the client? Do you think the client will like this?" And they all said, "Oh yes, the client is going to love this!"

All of a sudden, we were talking about feeling—how they were feeling about the pricing bid. But when we started, we just had our four pages of spreadsheets, the numbers, analysis, margins, gross margins, and operating costs. Sometimes you can be focused on the wrong things.

I feel like people miss it. They miss the whole point. It goes back to my opening question: *"How do you feel about that price?"* It goes straight to the heart, but it can also be a hard question to answer sometimes.

Here is a story my stepdaughter shared on a version of this lesson.

> Recently, I sat down to ask myself that question, and I realized that Doug would tell me to act in one of two ways when dealing with different situations—"Heart, Head, Heart" or "Head, Heart, Head." Doug has already touched on the importance of good communication. I think that his ability to use the "Heart, Head, Heart" approach when communicating is part of what makes him so successful. Especially when it comes to parenting. Growing up, I made plenty of mistakes. Whenever I was in trouble, Doug would begin his "scolding" with letting me know that he loved me. He would tell me what I did wrong, why it was wrong, and more often than not, the arguments would end with a hug. I can specifically think of a situation where I was so mad at my mom and Doug that I skipped our family dinner at Mesero's. I was being stubborn, and—even though I really wanted to be a part of the dinner—I could not bring myself to go. I eventually gave in and showed up to the restaurant—eyes still swollen and red from crying. Doug got up from the table and said: "I am so happy that you came. I do not like the way you spoke to your mom and me earlier, and when you stay at our house you should expect to follow our rules." Then he gave me a hug, ordered me a margarita, and the rest of the

dinner went perfectly smooth. Had Doug not taken this heart, head, heart approach, I could have easily gotten upset again and left the restaurant, or not have showed up to the dinner at all.

Doug also taught me the alternative to this approach—and it is one that I have had to utilize recently. My husband and I are currently house hunting. This can either be very fun or it can be very stressful, depending on how you choose to navigate the process. There have been many occasions where I have walked into a house and immediately said "I love it, let's buy it, let's make an offer!" BUT, if there is one thing my parents have ingrained in my head, it is to never buy something you cannot afford. This is where Doug's "Head, Heart, Head" comes into play. And after some frustrating and disappointing house visits, I decided to change to Doug's way of thinking. Mitchell and I figured out exactly the budget we can afford at our high and low end. We narrowed down the exact two neighborhoods where we wanted to buy a house. We determined what it is that we would "like" in a house and what it is that we would "need" in a house. Next, we went to see more houses. It was amazing how much more productive, less stressful, and fun it was to look at houses using my head and not my emotions! Mitchell was also very grateful, because he got tired of me saying I wanted to put an offer down on a house just based on how pretty the bathroom was or how big the closet was. Turns out that boring stuff like pipes, roofs, and insulation, are much more important in the long run.

CHAPTER 9:

COMMUNICATING TO CONNECT

*"The single biggest problem in communication
is the illusion that it has taken place."*
—GEORGE BERNARD SHAW

*"Good communication is the bridge
between confusion and clarity."*
—NAT TURNER

*"Communication to a relationship is like oxygen to life.
Without it, it dies."*
—TONY GASKINS

I have found that most people don't think through how they communicate—if they even think about it at all. Communication seems to be one of those things that should come easy, but communicating effectively can be very challenging work. In fact, most people just aren't very good at communicating.

Here's an example. Early in someone's career, they will not give their boss bad news, because they're afraid it's going to reflect negatively on them. Or they're afraid that if they do tell the boss something bad, they will get yelled at or will be in trouble. There's all this kind of "filtering" that people will do before they tell somebody something, to save themselves. It's not always self-preservation, but generally, it is. They use qualifiers in an attempt to shield themselves from any negative or unintentional blow-back.

It's the same as in baseball when a player says, "Well, we only lost by a run, right?" When no, they lost by not getting the other 22 men who were on base to score. The way you communicate a story of bad news or a loss, often seems to be out of a self-preservation mode or, in a way, to make yourself look good. So how should you communicate bad news or, harder still, receive it! The way that works for me is what I call "Think, Filter, Speak." (I understand there are many definitions of the word "filter." How I use this word below is not the engineering use of filter!)

Think, Filter, Speak ("TFS")

If someone uses a harsh word or critiques you, don't get defensive. Our natural tendency is to react when we feel threatened. Instead of trying to protect our image by entering self-preservation mode, we should use that opportunity to **think** about what is being said and **filter** our response before we **speak**!

This is one of the most important lessons in today's society and business environment. The ability to take in what has been said, read or viewed, filter the content, think about how or even *if* you want to respond, and then responding in the proper tone is invaluable. If you watch the news, political commentary, or your brothers and sisters in how they communicate, you'll see that we all need to learn this lesson.

When my daughter was interviewing with her law firm, one of the partners asked her what was the single most important lesson she had ever learned in life. To which she said, "My father taught me to think, filter, speak." She went through explaining the whole process of how when someone tells you something that offends you, you should first think about what their true meaning is. Then filter what you want to say back to them in your reply, and really consider how what you say will sound to the other person. Then, and only then, should you respond.

> It's not about manipulating people or telling them what they want to hear, it's about doing everything you can to make sure they hear what it is you truly want to tell them.

The "Think" part is reflecting on, "Okay, why have they said that to me." Then the "Filter" part is asking, "What's the best way to respond to them, so that I can get my point across as effectively as possible." It's not necessarily that you're trying to make a point to "one up" them, but instead, to really communicate your message effectively. Then you can "Speak" by responding accordingly. I think that lesson is really lost on many people.

I do see this a lot with experienced leaders. If I get hit by some stray comment, or get rubbed the wrong way in a meeting, the natural reaction is to get defensive. That's one of the worst reactions you can have. I think the practice of "Think, Filter, Speak" helps you take back control of your communication ability.

Caught in the Crossfire of Miscommunication

I had a difficult boss whose demeanor was strongly negative. A direct report of mine was having a hard time getting a project finished. My boss said to him, "You know, you never get anything done on time. How long is this going to take us?" My report's response, in turn, was very negative (preceded by a long pause with a blank stare). Finally, he said, "Well, everything just takes longer around here because of the environment in which we work." It had a negative and disrespectful connotation.

My boss was overreacting—the employee's work wasn't overdue all the time. But he was the boss, and he had a point, so he used that project as an example. My boss and my subordinate got into a very heated conversation. In reality, it was about one late project, just a misalignment about the original dates. But it really angered my subordinate and frustrated both parties. They had missed a great opportunity to connect with their communication and solve the problem. And I was in the crossfire.

None of that back and forth drama was very helpful for getting the project done anyway. It was just wasted energy and emotion. Not to mention, arguing with your boss's boss is generally a CLM (Career Limiting Move). Those are some of the negative consequences of poor communication.

Once things cooled off, I went back to this individual and coached him up on the wisdom of not arguing with someone who says something that's just so outrageously wrong, that they're smart enough to know what they said was inaccurate. There's no reason to point it out or make a fuss about it. I told him that if somebody said something like that to him again, to just let it fly by and redirect the conversation to talking about the specific project at hand. Then for him to make sure that he had all the data to back up his claims.

I explained that if he was missing a deadline, he could simply explain to the boss why. Maybe it was because of something that was out of his control. Or there was a contingency that was put into the agreement that was causing the project's delay. Whatever the reason, just explain it clearly. That way you've made sure that you are communicating on the main issue and addressing the relevant and helpful points—and not just reacting out of anger. Taking ownership of the delay—so you don't appear to be ducking responsibility—is also part of fixing it, but that is for another chapter.

An Example from Home

When my kids were younger, I traveled a lot for work. Sometimes when I'd go to discipline my daughter, she'd throw my hectic schedule up in my face and say things like, "How do you know, you're never around?" And I would reply back with, "Well, yes, Taylor, I've been home three nights out of five this week." I'd get the same kind of emotional outburst if I corrected her on missing curfew.

But I would recognize that she was just mad because I was disciplining her. That what she was saying really had no relevance to my authority as her father to discipline her. In other words, she felt attacked and was getting defensive. So, in turn, she was trying to make me upset.

I believe it all goes back to looking for the meaning behind the message and trying to understand first before being understood. It's also about taking into consideration the emotional impact of the words you use and carefully choosing how you respond. This is not easy, when someone—especially someone you love—tweaks your nose, it's hard not to react.

How Do They Process Information?

Another tip for effective communication is learning how your team members, boss, or loved ones process information. For instance, I work with a lot of people who are visual learners. They want to see the big picture first. That's how I am. I want to be told the problem or the answer right up front, and not have it buried in 14 pages of details and bullet points. I like to "see" the big goal right away. Others prefer to lead up to a conclusion, like a lawyer would present their case. Still others prefer to communicate with facts, stories, or word pictures.

Take my wife, for example. She talks adamantly and is very direct. Sometimes I ask her, "Are you mad at me?" because she's so point blank. But that's just how she speaks. That's normal for her. That's how she processes— adamantly. That's her calm. I need to consider her style when talking to her.

Knowing people's style will help you communicate with them more effectively.

"What Keeps You Up at Night?"

That's a famous question that came out of the consulting world about 15 years ago, and people still use it today. The point is to ask questions that get to the core issue. Whether it's with a person, a project, or a problem, ask "What's keeping you up at night?"

If somebody came up to me and said, "You know, you're just an awful person," or "Your team never performs well," or "Your division is behind again," I would sense there's something significant behind that kind of a comment.

That "something" is what's keeping them awake at night. That's the real issue. So what is *that thing?* What driving emotion is fueling that harsh comment or question? If you can deal with that emotion, or deal with that core issue that's driving the emotion, then I think you can get pretty far, pretty fast in finding a solution.

Tools to Understand Yourself and Others

Hiring managers or training and development departments utilize different personality assessments that can provide tremendous insight to how employees, or potential employees, think, act, and communicate. These tools can also be very helpful in learning how to deal with others, and they are continually used by larger corporations.

Take advantage of these resources, whatever they may be, to learn how to communicate more effectively. Many times, HR will have access to the DISC profile, Myers-Briggs, the Predictive Index, or the Emotional Quotient Index. Be sure to use those if you can get access to them.

I think tools like that give insight into the individuals you work with. These may be insights into your team members' propensity for taking action, how they handle conflict, or just how they tend to operate overall. Take the time to look at those results and understand them. There is a great deal of science behind assessments. Don't just write them off as fluff. You may find that there's a lot of interesting stuff in those assessments, and you might even learn a thing or two about yourself.

I remember an exercise where we were challenged as a group to solve a problem. It took us probably five times longer than it should have to solve this problem, but in the end, it was so much more of a complete solution, because all of our different viewpoints had been contributed. It's good to have some diversity on your team, to have different perspectives available to you, and to really know how to communicate with different people with different processing styles.

"Listening" to Body Language

The final point in communicating effectively is listening to what *isn't* being said. That means listening to what the *body* is saying. Develop the ability to read someone's eyes, their expressions, and their posture. Are they leaning in with understanding or leaning out in distraction? Are they actively listening like I described earlier, or just checking their phones or email. In face-to-face communication, you can tell when people are engaged or not.

That's part of the problem with texting and email. It's just a one-sided conversation that only happens when it is convenient for the sender. Instead, when you communicate in a conversation, you create a meaningful connection. You get to see how your words make an impact, and the recipient will physically respond.

That's important whether you're communicating with your boss, with your team, or with anybody else for that matter. Watching them react to what you're telling them helps you adjust your delivery to best communicate your message.

One of the many things that Doug has taught me is the importance of T.F.S. (Think - Filter – Act). He has a remarkable way of not looking at life's problems with a "this is not fair, let me pout about it" view — but a "let me take in this information, think about a way to solve it, and react in a calm and productive manner." Doug has proved on many occasions that the latter is a much more effective approach.

– TAYLOR WILLIAMS

Where can you apply this? When is the last time you did not use TFS? Where could it have come in handy? Are there people in your life for whom this would be helpful?

_____

_____

_____

_____

_____

_____

_____

_____

CHAPTER 10

LESSONS: THE VELCRO OF LIFE

"Life is a journey with problems to solve, lessons to learn, and most of all, experiences to enjoy."
—ANONYMOUS

"The meaning of life is discovered in the experience."
—ANONYMOUS

"Aside from Velcro, time is the most mysterious substance in the universe."
—DAVE BARRY

L ife is a learning process. Everything we learn and experience can provide us with a tremendous amount of insights to our own human nature. These insights give us a new perspective of our world and can help us relate to those around us.

But how do you create a *catalog* of all the lessons you have experienced? An index, if you will, that you can draw upon and remind yourself of a lesson learned the moment you need it?

Often, the lessons that we need the most are the ones we need when we are experiencing difficulty or a challenge. Maybe you have just received a poor performance review or have been written up by the boss. Or maybe you were asked to give a speech and failed miserably, or you did not get the grade you wanted. How do you take that negative experience and learn from it? How can you dissect it so that you see both the strengths and weaknesses of your performance?

Creating a Catalog of Experiences

Learning to draw lessons out of negative experiences (like the examples above) is one of the best ways you can start building your mental "catalog" of experiences. That way, the next time something bad happens, you can step back from the situation, recognize your error, and come away from the event having learned something.

When a situation comes up that is similar to one you've faced in the past, you have this mental catalog of lessons available to you. You can go back and think, *You know, the last time I tried this, it didn't go as well as I would have liked. I think I'll try something different.* When you analyze what went wrong and why it happened, you can learn from the situation and not ever have to repeat those same mistakes again. Remember earlier in the book when I discussed Edison's experience with the light bulb and finding a thousand ways it wouldn't work? Every single failure was an opening to learn and try something new.

A simple self-reflection exercise of asking, *What went well? What when wrong? And what could I do differently next time?* will give you insights to your failure and hope for improvement in the future. Be honest with yourself. Seek out folks who will be honest with you so you can learn, not just ones who will make you feel good. Folks who want you to be better—not just to be your friend. Teachers, coaches, and colleagues taught me most of the important lessons in my life.

Learning to Trust Your Gut

I understand that it can be hard at first to think about cataloging lessons, but after doing this exercise for a while, and looking at all of life as a learning environment, you will find that you can really begin to listen to the "lessons catalog" in your gut. In time, you will be able to trust your gut, because it has within it your active "catalog of experiences"—life lessons you can call upon when needed.

Maybe you have a big project due and some action items have fallen off the backburner. Your gut will remind you of those items in time to get them done for your project. Or maybe there's a big presentation you have to prepare for. If you trust your gut, you'll be able to thoroughly prepare for your presentation with plenty of time to spare. Listen to your gut and listen hard.

Sometimes in my career, I've jumped onto a conference call or gone into meetings without having done much in the way of preparation—though my gut told me to do so—and I've always immediately regretted it.

It's like when you find some leftovers in the fridge, and you can't remember how old they are. The best thing to do is not to eat it. Remember the phrase: *When in doubt, throw it out*? Well I've seen far too many people not throw it out, and their stomachs have paid for it. It's the same in business. They should have listened to their gut—*pun intended*.

Defining Wins and Losses

In life and in business, we tend to focus on earning the big "W." We want to win. Win that promotion, win the company sales challenge, and win that new account. On the flip side, we tend to get deflated with a loss. We're crushed if we lose a contest, a promotion, or a client. We second guess everything, we blame others, the environment, God, and even ourselves!

But I've learned that it's best not to focus too much on the excitement of victory, or conversely, on the agony of defeat. Rather, we should focus on learning from the lessons contained within *each experience* we have in life.

There is neither good nor bad in learning. It's all just learning. The lessons you learn are neutral. It's up to us and how we apply the lessons, that determines whether or not they are "good" or "bad." And sometimes this will require you to change your perspective.

> **Because an experience is an experience is an experience. You don't have to categorize it as either negative or positive. Just learn from it and take it for what it was—an experience you had.**

What experiences can you catalog right now? What did you learn? Write down the lesson no matter how painful.

_____

_____

_____

_____

_____

_____

_____

Look at Life Like a Piece of Velcro

I love Velcro. It's so convenient and such a helpful invention. It works great for kids who don't know how to tie their shoes, or for dog collars, or for keeping your lunch box closed.

But Velcro is also a great metaphor for life. If you look at life as a piece of Velcro, you will begin to see how all of your various experiences stick to you. Now the only question becomes, how can you bring those experiences— and the lessons within—back for your benefit when you need them the most?

This is how I do it. There are things in life that I'll really want to remember. Then there are things that I'll really want to understand. And still, there are things that are easy to just gloss over in my mind because maybe the memories are painful.

I find that sometimes going back and really thinking through what happened or what didn't happen, helps me to get motivated to do it the right way going forward. This is true whether you apply it to your job or finances or even weight loss and exercise. You can apply it to anything in life that requires you to "shift" your perspective. Instead of focusing on the good or bad, you can focus on learning and growth.

Lessons in the Lost Art of Public Speaking

One of the things that I really love to do is public speaking and communicating to a large group. Well if you really think about it, even at an individual level, this isn't just about communication or presentation, *it's about both*. The idea of doing a good presentation is kind of a lost art.

If you watch most people present, they stand up in front of a screen and talk to the slide. Then they click a button, and they turn around to look at the slide. Then there's an awkward moment of silence while their mind resets to what's on the slide. And then they either explain the points that you can already see on the slide, or they just read them verbatim. It's horrible! Ok, take a note here: The next time you see a presenter, keep one list of what you learned from their presentation and one list of how they presented. It does not have to be good or bad, but catalog what you liked about it, and it will help you down the road.

Even worse is when there's no headline, so you don't even know what they're talking about. And then there's no story. So essentially, the person presenting hasn't tuned the listeners' ears to what they're going to hear, and the audience has no idea what to expect. Because of that, the presenter has lost all opportunity for connection.

I've studied this a lot, and—through much trial and error—have taught myself how to be a better presenter. For instance, I always start with a headline. And this isn't the cliché formula: *Tell them what you're going to tell them. Tell them. And then tell them what you told them.* This is a real presentation formula that is both effective and empathetic to your audiences' needs.

You start with a headline such as "We had a great year," or "The reason we're doing this presentation is to make sure you guys know X." Then what I try to do is put the fewest slides possible in my slide deck, with as few words on them as possible, so that the audience can focus on me— not my slides. Then in my preparation, I write the headline on the slide, to make sure I make the headline.

Before I transition to the next slide, I write a transition sentence for myself in my notes, so that when I transition, I say, "Okay, now we're going to talk about the score card"—click—and now the audience is looking at the score card. I have tuned the listeners' ears to hear what they're going to see next on the slide, before they even see it. But this does one more very important thing, it tells your mind what comes next and automatically loads your brain with the dialog that goes with the slide. No awkward moment, no thinking about what you are going to say, it just flows!

I've learned in my catalog of life lessons, preparation is key. If I don't say this transition statement on each slide, or if I don't do the headline at the very beginning, then my presentation isn't going to connect. To present at my best and be able to interact with the audience, I want to have my presentation all squared away in order to not trip over my words. That's where having a catalog of lessons to draw upon becomes so valuable.

Getting Out of the Death Spiral

In my role in business, I often see someone making a series of bad decisions. Their poor judgment may put them into what I call a "death spiral," because so many times it just ends in destruction—damaged reputations, ended relationships, lost opportunity.

For example, say you're working with a client, and one of your deliverables on the numbers is not really what it should be. You've made the numbers up, or you rounded them up or down, to make it seem better. Well now you've just made a bad decision. You've manipulated the data for your benefit, not the client's. You've done this for your gain. Well, what if the client finds out, and you don't come clean? Now you have to make up another story about why you had to modify the data. And you end up having to tell a lie to cover your lie. Now you're in the death spiral. I see this all the time.

The death spiral doesn't just happen with lying about numbers, it also occurs when executives lose their tempers or co-workers drink too much at happy hour. There is always a choice to make a good decision or a bad one. Your catalog of lessons will be able to tell which is which.

> What I find, especially with younger people, is that they'll try to protect themselves, as opposed to just saying, "You know what, that was a really stupid decision. I modified the data. I won't do that again. I shouldn't have done that, and I'll just deal with the consequences." That's how you overcome the death spiral, you learn from those mistakes.

This kind of rationale doesn't just happen at the office. It can happen in your personal life. You can compromise in many areas—your health, finances, and relationships. One bad decision after another can lead you off your path and end up putting you in a hard spot. Whereas a series of good decisions can send you straight up the corporate ladder, and you can succeed while keeping your integrity.

Take Ownership

Taking ownership is all about taking responsibility for your life, for your career, and for your relationships. It's the realization that you are the "C.E.O of YOU." Just like admitting to your mistakes is the solution to overcoming the death spiral, taking ownership in life is the solution for becoming successful in any endeavor.

You can't blame your circumstances on someone else. You can't blame your problems on your boss, team member, or roommates. You have to be responsible for you. Taking ownership is all about living by the series of lessons you have learned in your life and becoming responsible for, and accountable to, your own dreams and desires.

Your life can't be dictated by a series of external events. If you don't like your employer, your housing situation, or something else, you can't wait for someone on the outside to give you a solution. You must make that change happen for yourself.

Once you take ownership over your life, it really helps put everything else into perspective, because then you become the master of your own journey.

Review and Adjust

Think about your own life. Where can you take more ownership of your situation? What don't you like that you need to change? And where have you not listened to your gut and had a negative consequence because of it?

Review the last month's activity and all of your significant events—both the "good" and the "bad." How can you reframe them all as neutral experiences?

Think of them like Velcro—these were just things that happened, experiences that you can learn from. Where was the silver lining? Where did something happen that you didn't expect to happen? What have you learned and what will you do differently next time?

Write those events down here, in shorthand if you are afraid someone else will read your notes, but take notes, think about them. This will really help.

_____

_____

_____

_____

_____

_____

I think God prepares us every day for what we have to do. My sense is that He doesn't give us anything we can't handle. So, whatever your challenge or obstacle is, you can handle it with good choices, and you can learn from it, "catalog" it, and you will remember how it makes you feel down deep.

Things will turn out ok. Sure, you're going to have experiences in life that are unpleasant. I used to have a huge problem with my finances. I thought I deserved one type of life, but my income was very different from my lifestyle. And rather than focusing on what I had and needed, I focused on what I did not have and wanted. The end of every month brought heartache and, to top it off, I was not honest with my family about what we really had the money to do. My inside ego wanted me to be the big shot who could afford anything, but my gut kept telling me I was just digging a deep hole.

That kind of behavior went on so long, and I was in so deep financially, that I finally went to God and asked for help as I was clearly powerless to change this part of my life. As I started to listen to Him and my gut, I made small improvements, spent less than I made, reduced my expenses, and lived within my means, I was much happier. Sometimes when you look back on life, you'll be able to see valuable lessons contained in those experiences. I have applied these key lessons about my ego, wants, income and status, to help me focus on what matters in life. Keep your perspective on growth and learning, and you'll become much happier and wiser because of it.

CHAPTER 11:

PERSONAL GOAL SETTING

"You are never too old to set a new goal or to dream a new dream."
—C.S. LEWIS

"Goals give you more than a reason to get up in the morning; they are an incentive to keep you going all day."
—HARVEY MACKAY

"A goal without a plan is only a dream."
—BRIAN TRACY

I'm passionate about personal goal setting. But unlike most other books on the topic of goals, I focus more on the *why* behind the goal. Your goal should motivate you, and if possible, serve others. You should believe in the benefits of achieving your goal. And the benefits of your goal don't just have to be about you. They can include benefits to your loved ones, your community, and your network.

You should be willing to learn new skills and adapt, if necessary, to reach your goal. When you really understand why you set a goal and lay out all the capabilities and the steps needed to achieve it, your mind and body will naturally buy into the goal. You should also write it down, as this enables your mind and body to work behind the scenes, subconsciously, to help you achieve your goal.

Goals Can Be Multifaceted

When I was just starting out in my career, my first set of goals, like many of my peers, were all focused around money and earning a position. I wanted to become a CEO, have a nice lifestyle, a fancy car, and a big house. I dreamed of a membership with a premier country club and the respect and admiration of all those who knew me. Oh yeah, and a hot wife!

> **But the why was lost on me—and literally, I mean, lost on ME! It was all about me—me, me, me, me, me. How I wanted to live, how I wanted to be viewed, and how much money I wanted to earn. But in reality, how would any of this benefit anyone else?**

Then, I learned the power of Zig Ziglar's quote: *"You can have everything in life you want if you will just help enough other people get what they want."* I began setting my goals to serve others. What I found is that when you set goals like that, it's so much more fun and fulfilling.

Once I started putting others in my goal statement, it carried a lot more weight. I had more of a commitment to stick with my goals. I did not want to let down others by not achieving these goals. My focus changed. Life became less about me and more about how I wanted to help others win.

I began coaching and mentoring people. I was committed to being there for my wife, my family, and my colleagues. Overall, my entire life took on more meaning. And if you ask my daughter, she would tell you I am a very slow learner in this area. Maybe you are too. Just stick with it! Society tends to bring it down to just a single aspect, or a view that is very linear. It becomes focused on what *I* can control or what *I* want to own.

Life isn't about reaching a certain title or income or about accumulating things. Rather it's about enjoying the process. It's about building healthy relationships and serving others. There are many books written on successful people who have attained all the material goals they could have ever dreamed of, but they felt hollow inside. If you help others meet their goals and reach yours in doing so, you will lead a very rich and rewarding life.

You can set a personal goal on many things, including those that we've discussed in this book. Things like learning to ask more questions, being more insightful, becoming a better presenter, or being more compassionate and faithful.

Goals can be professional or personal, health related or financial, spiritual or recreational. The point is, there's way more to life than just earning a fancy title and a high income.

Teams, Not Silos

Being in senior management, I get to help a lot of my team members set and achieve goals that are important to them. One of my goals as their boss has been to get our team to work so hard that not only do I get my direct reports promoted, but I get *their* direct reports promoted as well. This is not an easy task, but it is so rewarding when it happens.

This kind of "others-centered" goal setting makes me concentrate on the skills, capabilities, talents, and gifts of my team. I coach them up to the next level based on their own passions and level of performance. Just think about the ripple effect it has on my team members and their families once they are promoted because they had set goals, worked hard, and knew their why.

Something I really want to do in my role as Chief Operating Officer is to take divisions in the company that have historically been silos and transform them as unified teams. I want to take individuals who believe in advancing their own personal performance and make them care about contributing to the team more than they care about reaching their own personal goals. Think about a company that is more focused on being a team and helping each other rather than just asking "What's in it for me?" It's amazing what this type of performance environment can do for results and how much fun it is getting great results.

For me, the dynamic of how to do that is to create a team-friendly environment and then operate within that environment. I demonstrate through my leadership that the team is more important than the individual.

So, my personal goal is to create teams. It's not to be the CEO, it's not to get a bonus, and it's not to make more money. It's about asking, "How do I really build a team?" Whether I go on to become a consultant, speaker, board member, or I work in social services, I think putting together an effective team is really one of the most fun things to do in life. And the benefits flow, but the ones you feel are not as material.

When you work with an effective team, things happen faster. People are happy, and work is exciting. It is an interesting and fun environment to work in. So that's why I focus on improving individual team member's skills and capabilities to impact others—because it's not about the individual or about getting a title. It's about the team. And there is so much credit to go around that everyone feels fulfilled and cared about.

"When people who are actually creating a system start to see themselves as the source of their problems, they invariably discover a new capacity to create results they truly desire."
-PETER SENGE

Here is a story from a colleague who was helping our company with cultural change and how creating a team can help results.

> Doug has a unique ability to create, again and again, challenges for his people that demand that they collaborate and learn as a team to successfully navigate. He designs these so that individuals see and feel that when they take ownership individually and collectively, they are able to generate results they never thought possible. And when they achieve these results, they want and demand more opportunities like this from Doug. This sounds so much easier than it is!
>
> I watched Doug do this as his team struggled to figure out how to reduce the time it was taking to onboard enormous amounts of data. We are talking huge amounts of data and lots of time, upwards of 500 days. 500 days! Doug picked as—he likes to call it—"the longest pole in the tent", one area that was taking 250 days. For years the team was effective at incrementally reducing the time: 1 hour here and 10 minutes there. But Doug knew they could reduce more on the magnitude of 50%. He pushed *them* to set a goal—NOT HIM. He didn't tell them 50%, he asked them that if they were fully unleashed on reducing the on-boarding time how much could they reduce it? They, as a team, came up with 64%, beyond even what Doug thought was possible. Over the course of the next few months, the team came up

against seemingly intractable barriers and wanted to go back to the incremental expectations. Doug held the tension. Doug told them to keep striving for the goal they set of 64% and work together as a team and think fundamentally differently about how to generate these results. There was NO WAY an individual could have solved this; it demanded that they team in whole new ways. In just a few months and after many breakthrough ideas, the team reduced the time by 75%, beyond even what they originally thought possible. And now the team wanted more. So Doug opened the aperture and asked the larger organization to take on the entire onboarding process. And in just over a year, and after several rounds of these "opportunities," the organization grew by more than 30%. Where other leaders would have just told the team what to do and how to do it, Doug forced his people to come together as a team to drive results no one ever thought possible. Now the team can never go back to the way they worked before.

The Ladder and the Lattice

Goals have seasons. I'm in a different season than my team. I'm probably in a different season than you. So naturally, we will all have different goals that match each of our seasons. What I'm trying to do is open your perspective so that you can set personal goals differently.

One way I teach this is through the illustration of a lattice. Many people focus on climbing the corporate ladder, especially when they're young in their career. But life is more of a lattice. It's like a garden fence with crisscrossing patterns that go up, down, and sideways.

The idea is that, sometimes in life, you have to traverse up, and sometimes you actually have to traverse down. Or maybe you even have to go sideways. There are many different ways to reach your goals.

To use an earlier example, say you want to learn Spanish to help Spanish speaking people. You already know that you're going to be pretty crappy at Spanish for a while when learning it. But be ok with having to go through that whole learning process. Even though one of your skills is communicating, you may have to go "down" the lattice before going up while learning a new language. You will learn a whole new inflection process and a different way to emphasize what you say. You are stepping down in order to go up and get better at something new. You should be excited to try this and see if you can teach an old dog new tricks! Yo habla?

I've done this process throughout my career: going up and down, up and down— learning a new skill so I could move forward with my ultimate goal of helping others. Just look at my LinkedIn page.

I even did this when I was a management consultant. And then, when I went into running an IT shop, I had to do it again. Even though my degrees are in computers and mathematics, I wanted to learn different aspects of the business. When I took over part of the operations, I didn't have a lot of operational experience. So, as the leader, I was learning as much as I was teaching. I would turn my learning principles into team principles. That's taking the perspective of a lattice.

So again, instead of looking at your career as a straight ladder that you climb, consider it a lattice that you can traverse in different directions, as needed. Think about all the things you can learn and experience! You can have great fun in taking this approach to your career.

Seasons of Short, Medium, and Long-Term Goals

As your seasons change in life, so will the goals you set. Maybe you'll need to set a short-term or medium-range goal. Maybe you're looking at the longterm. The type of goal changes with the season you are in.

Short-term goals are for immediate wants and needs, typically within the next six to nine months. They might be a year, year and a half, or less. I call them "calendar goals" because you can count down the days and measure progress as you go along.

If you're a mid-level manager struggling to hit your numbers or to get your team to operate cohesively, then your short-term goal deadline might be by the end of the quarter. It all depends on your season in life and what is important to you.

Medium goals are in the two-to-five-year range. So again, learning a new language and other skill-focused or transitional goals are in the medium-term range. These tend to take more discipline and some type of milestone, so you'll know if you are progressing at the right rate. Like writing this book—I wanted to do it for years. My coach pushed me to start putting things on paper, attend a book-writing workshop, and get to it!

Long-term goals could be anything ten years or longer. If you're a young 20-something just starting your career, your long-range goal might be to retire at 60. That's 40 years away! I love to use the line if you are looking back at great success and have achieved all your goals, what did you achieve? How will you be remembered and how does your legacy live on?

_____

_____

_____

_____

_____

_____

Transition to Teaching

I have a mid-term goal that I will retire in the next few years. I have a clear vision of what I want my retirement to look like. I know that I may never fully retire, but I don't want a full-time job. I'm going to teach.

> My teaching is probably not going to be in a classroom, it's going to be corporate based. I want to look at being an executive chair and teaching other executives how to operate some of these businesses effectively.

If I'm setting these goals up and what I want to do is teach, then, there is a certain set of skills, capabilities, and networks I need to build to be able to reach that goal.

Getting Crystal Clear on Your Goals

As you think about your own life, think about the kind of life you are creating. What pieces of your goal do you need to put into place right now in order to execute on your short, medium, and long-term goals? How can you help others reach their goals? What is important to you in this season?

The key to personal goal setting is to know the *why* behind your goal. Be sure it is focused on your larger purpose and that it serves others. Knowing those expectations can help you understand what you need to get done in order to reach your goal. You'll have a greater commitment to make it happen.

The important part is having a crystal-clear goal that you can create an action plan for achieving. Then you must execute your plan in order to turn your goal into a reality. What I have learned is that most people don't really think about setting goals like this.

Footprints in the Snow

I remember when I was really young, my dad took me out in the snow and stood me up against a tree. He said, "What I want you to do is walk a straight line by putting your heel to toe, heel to toe. And I want you to walk to that other tree across the yard. But I don't want you to look at that second tree. Instead, I want you to look at your feet. I want your feet to be as straight as possible: heel to toe, heel to toe, just keep looking at your feet."

So, I did that. And, of course, I had to peek up every now and then to see where I was going and where the tree was. When I finally got to the other tree and I looked back, I could see how my path wasn't a straight line at all.

It was all wavy and strayed back and forth. I had all these different types of variations in the size of my gait and different angles in my footprints because I really didn't know where I was going. I was kind of walking blindly. Even though I had a plan and a direction, and I tried to keep my feet straight, when I looked back at my tracks in the snow, I could see that my path had been very crooked.

But after that exercise, my dad turned me around and said, "OK. This time, I want you to walk back to the first tree. But I don't want you to look at your feet at all. Instead, I just want you to look at the tree."

So, I walked back to the first tree without looking at my feet at all. And when I reached the tree, I turned to look back and saw that my path was perfectly straight. My footprints in the snow were in a straight line, no sidesteps at all. So what does that tell you?

It tells you to focus on your goal and reaching your destination. Don't be concerned if you veer off course a little. If you focus on your path, you'll get further and further off course. Focus on reaching your goal; you will be sure to arrive at it in time.

Enjoy the Walk

As I prepare to leave you in these last few pages, I want to help you think about your "why" and remember to use the lessons in this book to enhance your perspective, or to help you hone your perspective—or maybe even to SHIFT your perspective.

I hope to have given you little glimpses and insights into what success, meaning, and fulfillment look like for me. I have shared with you some meaningful lessons that I've collected along the way. I believe that the journey is so much more interesting than the destination.

How Will You Define Success?

This goes back to how you defined success earlier in the book. Has that definition changed now that you have finished these lessons? Has your perspective shifted in any way?

I would like to ask you, have you declared success in each of these areas? I think if you really work on each of these areas, you will be able to declare success, and you'll ultimately experience success in life in a much bigger way. You will become a better person—better at asking questions and listening. I think that following this advice will make you better at life overall.

I hope you see this book as a reference manual, if you will, for shift gears in life. You can come back to this book every couple of years and see how you previously answered the questions at the end of each chapter, how you would answer them now, and then gauge yourself on what you've learned, what you can improve, or where you have taken ground. You may even find that you have identified some weak areas where you are stagnant and need more work. Whatever it is, it is up to you.

I don't mean to give you any answers. That's not the point. My goal is to get you to consider your perspective and to learn a new or different way of looking at things. To consider a problem or situation and think differently about how you can use your unique skills and experience to find the solution.

I hope I have given you the tools to shift your perspective. Because ultimately, I think reading a book like this improves your outcome. If you master these skills, and they become more conscious for you, it will make you a more interesting, thoughtful, and successful person. So go ahead, SHIFT!

NOTES

Chapter 1

[1] C. Richard Weylman, *The Power of Why: Breaking Out in a Competitive Marketplace*, (New York, New York: Houghton Mifflin Harcourt Publishing Company, 2013), 4.

[2] Simon Sinek, *Start with Why: How Great Leaders Inspire Everyone to Take Action*, (New York, New York: Penguin Group, 2011), ix.

Chapter 2

[1] History.com editors, *Thomas Edison*, history.com, updated June 6, 2019, https://www.history.com/topics/inventions/thomas-edison.

[2] Lauren Albe, *The History of Airbnb*, telegraph.co.uk, December 1, 2015, https://www.telegraph.co.uk/technology/technology-video/ 12021531/the-history-of-airbnb.html.

[3] Jessica Salter, *Airbnb: The story behind the $1.3bn room-letting website*, the telegraph.co.uk. September 7, 2012, https://www.telegraph.co.uk/technology/news/9525267/Airbnb-The-story-behind-the-1.3bn-room-letting-website.html.

Chapter 3

[1] Christopher Benek, *God can be found in difference between happiness and joy,* islandpacket.com, October 7, 2014, https://www.islandpacket.com/living/religion/article33609807.html.

CPSIA information can be obtained
at www.ICGtesting.com
Printed in the USA
BVHW041752240220
573162BV00007B/703